Walk With Me

God's Call to the Church
and All Who Hear

by

Annette Bryans

WESTBOW
PRESS®
A DIVISION OF THOMAS NELSON
& ZONDERVAN

WestBow Press books may be ordered through booksellers or by contacting:

WestBow Press
A Division of Thomas Nelson & Zondervan
1663 Liberty Drive
Bloomington, IN 47403
www.westbowpress.com
844-714-3454

Cover art copyright June Corry, used by permission.
Cover author photo by Kim and James Bryans, used by permission.
Interior illustrations by Rob Lassetter, Lassetter
Studio, LLC, copyright Annette Bryans.
Photo pg 236 copyright Annette Bryans

Scripture quotations are taken from The New American Standard Bible®, Copyright © 1960, 1962, 1963, 1968, 1971, 1972, 1973, 1975, 1977, 1995 by The Lockman Foundation. Used by permission.

ISBN: 978-1-6642-9472-1 (sc)
ISBN: 978-1-6642-9474-5 (hc)
ISBN: 978-1-6642-9473-8 (e)

Library of Congress Control Number: 2023904529

Print information available on the last page.

WestBow Press rev. date: 04/05/2023

Walk With Me

God's call to the church is to walk with Him through the poetic beauty of Life's Journey. He summons all who hear to travel the pathway in loving reply of commitment.

Within the designed plan from the foundation of the world, the Journey walk together reveals the Path of Life. The Genre Steppingstones represent the Life Path, as the charted course guides those who aspire to search for Security.

The milestone points of progression in Spiritual growth offer a new perspective toward the benefit of the daily walk with Him forever.

As the Journey quest appears nearing attainment for assurance of Security, anticipation heightens to reach another plane filled with joy. To proceed promises The Journey story is continuous.

The Designed Plan was established as God desired; man's need is met and the resource is available for completion. The Preparation Purpose enables the aspiring one to enjoin His effort toward the wondrous works of God displayed in Genre.

Dedication
For Commitment to Service
To Amanda Bryans
To Craig Bryans

With loving gratitude my expression of thanksgiving is an offering of praise for your gifts of time and skill. Your genuine interest in this inspired endeavor is exceedingly joyful to me.

The Genre order is an answered prayer Amanda and I share. Typing the collection of poetic verse is another joining of effort and resources to assign Title to each class.

Diligently Craig assumed responsibility to continue the work in progress. Faithfully his technical experience contributed to the completion of <u>Walk With Me</u>; God's Bidding to Journey with Him along the Path of Life.

Dedicated
To Camille Lassetter

Within appreciation for our unique friendship, I offer to you my heartfelt gratitude for your kindness and loving compassion. It is a pleasure to share the utmost enjoyment gleaned from the experience in writing <u>Walk With Me</u>, God's call to the church. Thank you for your gift of expertise and commitment of immeasurable time investment. The personal interest expressed frequently is held in the treasury of memory with warmest regard.

Dedicated To Friends Dearly Ready to Share, Who live out 1 Timothy 6:18, Whose Hope is in God. He Gives Good Things For Our Joy.

June Corry's sharing her beautiful painting of the church. The pathway first leads to the welcoming door, then beyond to ministry beyond the church. Turning to follow, the path leads to ministry beyond the church. In kind, Jesus fed the multitude on the mountainside.

Carolyn Warner's ministry of genuine interest in the well-being of others leads her in faithfully time offered service. Valuable experience, nor love can be measured in time. Blessings are received with gifts. Crowns are graciously adorned.

Elyse Bryans' enthusiastic reply to complete a task is frequently contagious. Sharing her zest of enjoyment is a blessing for all known to her. Elyse's very being represents her gift of joy. The loving heart rejoices.

Joyce Crowder's prompt reply to accept a term of service is very gratifying. Her cheerful attitude always lifts my heart. This friend attentively also fosters inspiration for everyone within her own pathway encounter. Each day is a journey of discovery.

Sara Eubank's ministry of affirmation effected a resurgence of attention to the purpose predetermined for writing. Therewith, insight increased, and the implanted word revealed clarification. Mighty harvests appear from tiny seeds planted.

Family

Within the depth of my heartfelt love, I pen these words to my God given family. Your love, and faith, and especially your inmost precious oneself in name, has filled my life with joy. Each of you has a place reserved of endearment in my life.

It is in appreciation, and with sincere gratitude for your sharing your life and your wisdom, that my gain is greater insight and understanding. May you indeed increase in favor and pleasure with the Lord.

As heirs of God and fellow-heirs with Christ, hear the call to "forever <u>Walk With Me</u> along the Path of Life."

Family Dedications

To our family with inmost love to share my experience of the daily walk with God. Within the penned recording of this inspired endeavor, hear God's resounding call to each of you by name.

"Walk With Me along the Path of Life
that has been made known to you."

For my valued treasure, held within the heart's assigned space for our family circle. Each one a contributing gifted link of connection completes the harmonious unity.

Elyse, who promptly recalls the word in scripture to claim God's promise.

Craig, always ready to assist meeting a need, and sharing his testimony.

Kim receives assurance from the Bible and taking the word inward to her heart.

Amanda, compassionately responds to need perceived, and extends an offer to help.

James' experience of God's Spirit making His presence known to him continues.

Luann gives her praise offering, and leads others in worship and serving.

Catie expresses her belief in fairness and support for those who deserve equity.

Ben is strong in recognizing the benefit in character building.

Don's caring and encouragement since childhood continues ministering to many.

Bob, remembrance brings forth loving memories for Bob's mindful awareness of Jesus' teaching in the Holy Bible. It was always confirming to our children, and to my hearing their Dad's sharing his belief in life's principles from the word of God. Quoting scripture, Bob ministered to his family through teaching.

Family Commemoration For Robbe Bryans

Love of inmost depth and dearest affection bring to mind the glowing remembrance of **Robbe**.

Beloved, respected, and commended in steadfast character, his gift of life, beneficial to others and shared by many, has been a gifted blessing to each of his family.

We remain therefore to join before the risen Lord Jesus to praise and bow together in worship. God's love perfected.

Acknowledgments

To all our friends, partners in prayer,
who have joined together and interceded for me in prayer.

Acknowledgment

With gratitude for our friends pursuing guidance to step forward in the way of peace.   gleaned from Psalm 34:14, Luke 1:79

Peggy cheerfully responds to greetings and to calls of more definite inquiry. She is gracious in offering service and always demonstrating abundant kindness. Truly Peggy is a teacher and walks in a manner worthy of the Lord.

Carolyn has experienced ministering in areas of service to others. She has worked in fields of public service that introduced her to friends as well as opportunity to minister. How pleasant are our places the Lord has provided.

Laura is truly diligent to the task at hand, remains to serve and assist where there is a need. She is a prayer partner in every sense of the word, and faithful in time of adversity or rejoicing.

Sue, having walked the well traveled pathway of sorrow, reaches out within her heartfelt compassion. Sue's own pain propels her sharing Christ's sufferings with those the Lord assigns to her ministry.

To all our friends and prayer partners who have joined me, and have interceded for me. For **Mary, Nancy, Elizabeth, and Yvonne**, I extend my loving gratitude for your visits. Sharing our time of the inmost painful loss shall remain one of the dearest memories treasured. your thoughtfulness and gifts of time and love are precious, as those received from our other friends and loved ones.

Kay is a blessing. Prepared to share her testimony, she is attentive in the exchange of sharing. As well as an instrument of faith forwarding the good news, Kay follows the resounding call to serve.

Mary is the envisioned pleasantries of years in time. As a beacon of hope during an eventful farewell, she very quietly ministered. Passing seasons bring Mary's continuous gift of sharing her life.

For **Cova Jane**, whose heart enmeshed with my heart each day for thirty years within the precious privilege of intercessory prayer. May our Lord continue to bless you as insight is bestowed through obedience to scripture, believing He answers when two agree as touching asking in Jesus' name.

June, so uniquely placed in my life. Led by the Holy Spirit, obediently followed the Lord's prompting to share with me God's promise for a special presentation. We, unaware at the time, reserved the intuitive "God has something for you," until realization confirmed that preparation was made for Our Heavenly Father's inspirational gift of self-expression fulfilling His Purpose to follow His direction.

Yvonne, for your genuine enthusiasm, and sincere interest in our aspiring together <u>to press on toward the goal for the prize.</u> Thank you for the hours together breaking bread, searching the scriptures, and administering the application of medicinal laughter.

God's gift of beauty in the name **Grace** extended beyond my initial comprehension of God's many aspects of His grace. Through our sharing life's areas of work, and family, the discovery and depth of new meaning for friendship, support, and learning God's word has become very important. Moreover, new light shines upon love, grace and wisdom within scripture.

Joyce's love and our missing our Mothers together holds the special place in my heart. This dear counselor, steadfast, and encouraging, shall always move within her ministry of caring for others, speaking spiritual truth with boldness and confidence. Thank you for attentive concerns and an alternate perspective wrapped in loving kindness.

Sara's embracing the Lord's gifts of initiative, ministry, and other blessings gives hope to those directed. Hiding His word in her heart to please our Lord, and her genuine concern for many among whom I have known, this lasting friendship is a treasure.

Carol, sensitive, strong in faith, and portraying loyalty endears your entire family to everyone who knows and loves you. My joy is to have met you, find our mutual deepening love for the Lord and appreciate your concern for your own influential testimony for God's enriching your life abundantly.

Martha, how sweet your peaceful countenance becomes encouragement to reaffirm my faith in believing God's Holy word a directive to recall Christ gives His peace to all.

Joann: attentive and sincerely sympathetic to a broken heart. A shining example of sharing Jesus' Suffering, and learning submissiveness to the Will of God, has ministered to me. Thank you for sharing the experience of the sweet Holy Spirit.

To all my classmates who accepted me when I entered their established friendship group. Bless these adoptive, caring, loving persons who have maintained contact and concern for my life lo these many decades.

Pat, teacher in many areas. My joy has been to learn your value placed upon friendship, and constant awareness for the needs of others. I am honored to have been counted one as special to know your family.

Carolyn, attentive, patient and sacrificial in offering assistance frequently. Faithfully a disciple of servitude, as well as a continuous concern for friends' unresolved state of distress.

Pastor Commemorative

Reverend W.T. Booth visited with my family in our home when I accepted Christ as personal Lord and Savior. He encouraged me to follow Jesus' example in Believer's Baptism by immersion.

Doctor Walter E. Sanders pastored the first Church my husband and I joined when we married. We began our Christian journey in the Married Young People's Department with friends who have remained especially dear to our hearts.

Doctor Kenneth Z. Ellison led the Mission from Roswell Street Baptist to become ordained as the Eastside Baptist Church in six months with the Charter Membership numbering sixty-two. Soon his family's ministry was directed to the Foreign Mission Field in Indonesia for thirty-five years. Presently Ken and Mary continue serving our Lord upon their return to Eastside and the widely surrounding areas.

Doctor O.M. Siegler became our interim pastor and ministered to our congregation with wisdom and committed years of service dating before, as long ago to my knowledge, as when his preaching ministered to my Grandfather Bannister at Sandy Plains Baptist.

Reverend Arnall Richardson responded to God's call to shepherd Eastside fellowship and serve in his ministry to the Marietta community. He dedicated his heart and time to our Church and to personal needs reaching his attention.

Reverend Justus Garrett became our fourth Pastor following the death of Reverend Arnall Richardson. Through Reverend Garrett's pastorate other members and I, learned that God anoints those whom He elects.

Doctor Clark G. Hutchinson ministered to the increasing membership of Eastside with his family and his focus extended, and encompassed far reaching distances beyond our Church family. He ministered to my personal need during the death of my Dad, extending his interest to expand the distance crossing many miles of our country.

Doctor Gerald Harris, Senior Pastor of Eastside Baptist, continued as those before, proclaiming the Word of God. Ministering where needed and expressing personal interest to each person he meets, Our Lord's Gospel Message has reached many through the enabling Power of the Holy Spirit.

Doctor David Chauncy, Senior Pastor of Eastside Baptist Church followed Doctor Harris.

Doctor John Hull, currently serving as Senior Pastor of Eastside Baptist Church.

Preface

<u>Walk With Me</u> - God's Call to the Church is the wonderful story of my life committed to the daily walk with the Lord God. The resounding call heard was familiar, for God has spoken through His Word in Holy Scripture. Clearly known within the heartfelt inner being, God shared His words of love and direction for me.

As the story opens, it is revealed that there are many aspects intermingling, contributing to the life and ministry of my commitment to walk with God. The Living Story appears to fill the pages for a picture of my life's testimony, a fabric which is woven together with the durable yarns of love, faith, trust, obedience and commitment. A Living Story that is written and recorded within my life's journey.

The story of one whose character is by name, Annette. While walking with God along the pathway throughout the journey of life, an unfolding of my story continues.

The spiritual growth within the experiences and events encountered as the daily walk continues and appears enlightened. Therein God's foreknown plan of the charted course leads toward the quest for security.

Inspired to further seek the Lord's wisdom, the search ensues. He directed my interpreting His words by leading my way through scripture references. God pointedly directed the written verse in prose to me from the Word of God.

Introduction

*Thou wilt make known to me
the path of life.
Thy word is a lamp to my feet
and a light to my path.*

Psalm 16:11a, Psalm 119:105

God's call to the church, <u>Walk With Me</u>, is a poetic account compiled from the personal experiences gleaned through the spiritually inspired words in scripture. The verses and essays previously written express the predetermined meaning of the poetic aspect regarding beauty.

Through prayerful direction, the Genre series order is in place. For the poetical collection divisions, a Genre is assigned and entitles each group or class of poetry which pertain to beauty.

The Genre order, twelve count, is an eight phase design for joining the Tri-fold plan to complete the intended purpose. God's desire to share in the daily walk unfolds the creative purpose. To chart the meaning and understanding of the Path of Life, and the Journey Security quest; and Preparation readiness for the Presentation, comprise God's Purpose to impart His intended desire.

Tracing the Genre order beginning with the first division entitled Love, the Purpose Plan opens. The Plan view reveals the Path of Life represented as the Genre steppingstones. A course guideline is charted, clearly seen to follow the plan toward the goal.

The fathomless depth of God's Love precedes the Preparation Plan purpose. The continuous overflowing Love nourishes the implanted word of God.

Love is positioned as first in the Genre series as appearing in a visual to depict the beauty in grand motion. An envisioned picture guards the artistic scenery for review. The Waterfall of Love cascading over each steppingstone experience isn't easily perceived. Only the audible force permeating the gift of Love with same brilliance and wonder mindfully retained.

Life's continuous Preparation, a segment of the Purposed Plan, was established to make ready for the assurance of Security. To comprehend the desired gifted Legacy Purpose from the beginning, God intended the Inheritance obtained to be made known. Likewise the Path of Life is made known through the daily walk.

In His grace and mercy God predestined the born again to obtain the Inheritance that is imperishable. The Legacy Inheritance segment extends and encompasses the heirs of God. As children of God we are heirs of God, and we are fellow-heirs of Christ.

Numerous phases comprise each Purpose Plan, including God's work in you for His will and pleasure. This work, in Milestone experiences, equips and prepares for The Presentation which is so eagerly anticipated.

The wealth of the designed pattern in the Fabric of Life awaits the connecting threads of works evidenced. The means by which the Lord accomplishes this work, may be considered as follows.

Genre

Purpose - To Accomplish:

Walk With Me - Path of Life- Assurance of Security

Phase - To advance the Path of Life Journey toward preparation

Legacy - Inheritance

The Genre series is ordered to reveal the poetic aspect of beauty. As the plan opens and the phase design unfolds, the intended purpose to fulfill is accomplished.

Each one of the series is designated as a stone for stepping in sequence to move forward in the daily walk commitment.

A reserved display of creative works of wonder appear throughout the Genre order. As the phase of preparation joins the wondrous works with the works equipped, God's own plan continues. The weaving of works enhance the Fabric of Life. In kind, the Fabric design emerging lends beauty to the Tapestry of Life.

The intricately designed pattern of the Life Tapestry shall remain continuously treasured among God's pleasure.

The Genre steppingstones represent The Path of Life. The sequence connection order becomes the stone path side to walk along the charted course.

The steppingstones number twelve within the series order. Each Genre stone is a portrayal of special contribution toward the intended search for Security. The Path of Life Journey records the Living Story revealed in the Tapestry of Life.

The Genre order entitles the Division that is assigned to the class of poetic verse and prose. Each selected class of verse is an expression of beauty within the topic and title of the same name.

Milestone points of works appear for experiencing the progression of spiritual growth.

Love is positioned as first in the Genre order. Imagery allows the visual of Love overflowing each stone and the experience of God's work amid the life walk. Love is continuous, as God's purpose is continuous, and everlasting. God is Love and bids the walk with Him eternal.

(Note: At the beginning of each Genre there is a contents informational page listing bible verses of inspiration for you to explore on your own, as well as the titles of poetic verse to follow.)

Genre Title Divisions

Walk With Me

Walk in love just as Christ also loved you and gave Himself up for us, an offering and a sacrifice to God.

Ephesians 5:2

Walk With Me.....

Along the life path made known to you for the beauty of wisdom yet revealed and held for times in understanding.

Together following the steppingstones toward the aspired goal of security.

To encounter the journey course, a charted guideline within a Tri-fold Plan.

Experiencing the eight aspects of the Genre purpose to prepare for the Presentation.

Committed to pursue the Genre Love position, as the Waterfall cascading over each Genre steppingstone of life. Likewise, the implanted word is nourished from the Love overflow.

Living the Journey Story

Living the Journey Story

The Genre series is ordered to reveal the poetic aspect of beauty. As the plan opens and the phase design unfolds, the intended purpose to fulfill is accomplished.

Each one of the series is designated as a stone for stepping in sequence to move forward in the daily walk commitment.

A reserved display of creative works of wonder appear throughout the Genre order. As the phase of preparation joins the wondrous works with the works equipped, God's own plan continues. The weaving of works enhance the Fabric of Life. In kind, the Fabric design emerging lends beauty to the Tapestry of Life.

The intricately designed pattern of the Life Tapestry shall remain continuously treasured among God's pleasure.

The Genre steppingstones represent The Path of Life. The sequence connection order becomes the stone path to walk along the charted course.

The steppingstones number twelve within the series order. Each Genre stone is a portrayal of special contribution toward the intended search for Security. The Path of Life Journey records the Living Story revealed in the Tapestry of Life.

The Genre order entitles the Division that is assigned to the class of poetic verse and prose. Each selected class of verse is an expression of beauty within the topic and title of the same name.

Living the Journey Story
Imagery

The story of one's life is a wonderful Journey following the Path of Life. The path course is charted to reach God's purpose. Thereby the Kingdom of His Beloved Son, and The Legacy-Inheritance plans are fulfilled within purposed timing.

The Journey story begins as God consecrates the new born baby, setting the precious new life aside for a special ministry. Proceeding from the moment of birth our heavenly Father initiates His works to commence in the child. In purpose and appointed time, the Path of Life is made known, and the call is heard to <u>Walk With Me</u>.

A response in loving commitment prefaces the forthcoming experiences throughout the life Journey. The eventful happenings are noteworthy to enhance the poetic beauty pervading the story of life God perceived from the Beginning.

Throughout the Journey of Life, experiences of Milestone progression are encountered. Each phase of spiritual growth becomes an important aspect of the written story.

The Genre order of the Life path preserves God's wondrous works displayed. The Titled stories, of which there are twelve, express the works of wonder within the area in kind.

Echoes of Creation proclaim the purpose of all that is eternal is everlasting. The Love of God overflowing, and moving within the experiences of the Journey. Through Christ's atoning blood on the Cross, there is Life eternal.

Forward

I press on toward the goal for the prize of the upward call of God in Christ Jesus.

Philippians 3:14

Continue stepping along the stone path of Genre for the Journey advancement toward the Legacy-Inheritance purposed before the foundation of the world.

The Charted Course is marked Forwarding. The Preparation Plan is continuous in design, as well as purposed for completion.

Aspirations to attain Security, seemingly become quite near. The pent desire ever so close at hand, is as touching the sought after prize.

Prompted to exert every effort to forge ahead, finds the reserved treasure is wrapped in the wealth of Love.

Turn the page, as opening a door. To step upon the path of life's stone walk is to continue the journey seeking all which God has prepared for those who love Him.

Living the Journey Story

Once again the resounding call is heard to walk with the Lord. To traverse the steppingstone Path of Life throughout the charted Journey. Therein the eventful experiences reveal the poetic beauty purposed for the story of one's life.

The colorful, uniquely shaped pathway visibly appears, as the steppingstone course is charted to stretch beyond viewing distance. The well trodden steps along the Journey reach points of Milestone progression for spiritual growth.

One of God's own paths made straight is the distinguished walk of the steppingstones. Each stone is appropriately named, displaying the wonders worked within the same named area.

These works of wisdom and inspiration enhance the foreknown experiences for shaping the story. The purpose is to illustrate the many aspects of beauty in love, as God designed the creation of life in mankind.

Entitlement as Topics aid in stepping forward to envision the story taking form. Each preface heightens the anticipation of turning pages that reveal the works join to shape the story.

Lift the page to continue the steppingstone journey. The turning of pages bring forth imagery of the story evolving as an artistic wall hanging. This handwoven Tapestry of Life becomes visible for viewing in purposed timing. A beautiful design of one's life.

Love

Walk in love, just as Christ also loved you, and gave Himself up for us, an offering and a sacrifice to God.

Ephesians 5:2

Waterfall of Love
Imagery View

Overflowing the experiences along the Path of Life as the Love of God calls, <u>Walk with Me</u>.

The steppingstone Path of Life appears beneath the magnificent Waterfall of Love. God's Love gift for flowing throughout each stone enhancing the experiences within the entitled areas. The distinctive and hued coloring and uniquely shaped stones allow the shade of light to display the engraved Name of each steppingstone.

As the Falls of Love are continuous in their rushing purpose and sound of mighty force, the steppingstone Path is charted; to follow as the course guideline for leading every step to Journey with the Lord.

The fathomless depth of Love is a continuous overflowing beauty to enhance each steppingstone along the life path.

The Waterfall of Love with a rushing sound, is purposed to flow throughout the engraved named stone path, to cover every step toward the assurance of eternal security.

The straying streams of vapor mist, from the mighty force of the waterfall, enhance the experiences of progression in spiritual growth.

The Waterfall of Love portrays the Love of God, for God is Love.

As the depth of Love is continuous the cascading beauty of Love forever flows. To move throughout the experiences of life's path and in the Journey walk. Love in all splendor remains within the heart, daily walking with God.

Love of God
Everlasting

LOVE

Know My Love		Genesis 1:25
Hear My Word		John 5:24
Learn From Me	Take My Yoke Upon You	Matthew 11:29
Love	God Is Love	Deuteronomy 6:5

LOVE UNCONDITIONAL

LOVE LETTERS FROM GOD*   To Uniquely Created   Psalms 71:6

    CHOSEN COMPANION
    PROVISION
    APPEAL FOR TRUTH
    PROMISES
    COMMITTED TO SLUMBERING ONE
    EXPECTATIONS- HOPE
    RESPONSE- MY DELIGHTFUL LOVE
    LOVE OF MY HEART
    A SPECIAL DELIVERY

WHAT IS A NAME

Desired Favored Above Silver and Gold	Proverbs 22:1
A Good Name Is Better Than Ointment	Ecclesiastes 4:1

*See preface pg 23

LOVE UNCONDITIONAL

In the beginning was the Word
The Word was with God
Eternity Past
The Word was God infinitely
Everlasting.

Holy purpose established in preparation
To entreat man's heart to receive
God's ordained love assigned universal legacy
The spoken Word effected
Creation into being.

The heavens, earth, and seas appeared
Though none afore existed to behold.
Unfolding love reached limitless boundary
Transcending mortal's extent of contemplation
Occupying minute particles of space
Incomprehensibly.

"Let us make man in Our Image."
Thus, love provisional perceived
Man's need for a help meet.
Family and fellowship communion
With the Creator ensued.

LOVE LETTERS FROM GOD
CHOSEN COMPANION

Dear one I have loved you before the beginning of time
With the immensity and depth
That is wider than the universe
Farther reaching than any fathomless sea.

Greater than the imagination of the
Heavens.
Initiating the perfection of my adoring affection
You were known before formation
Creation, and Birth.

Crowning the original conceptions of the unique person
Identified as yourself
The Word was spoken in unison
Recorded in Genesis 1:26
"Let us make man in Our Image."

Fashioning my only Son's Bride
The most beautiful, lovely body
Presented to express the Majestic Heart of God
My chosen Love
The Church.

My sacrificial desire established
For you to choose My love in return.
Thus, divinely the most magnificent
Love Story Ever.

All creation, male, female, and surrounding
Heavens and Earth
Proclaimed
"It is very good."
The First Covenant
My chosen companion
My chosen love
Purpose accomplished within completion.

LOVE LETTERS FROM GOD
PROVISION

My Dear Love
Provided is every need and desire of pleasantry
As given dominion over every living thing upon the earth.
A Second Covenant bestowed as loving gift.

My heart is broken from the pain of grief
The betrayal of your unbelieving rejection.
The First Covenant shattered through spiritual separation
And sinful deception.

I have designed you, your every need
Do not doubt Me. Do not try Me.
My Word is True. My Word is Pure.
Consequential experience is imminent
Within my laws. My Commands. My Covenants.
My plans endure forever the purpose of My Heart
Through all generations.

Adam formed from dust from the ground became a living being
From my very own breath of Life.
Eve was given to her husband,
For she was taken from his flesh and bone
Placed by his side to fulfill the eternal purpose of mutual love and respect.
Presenting the picture of God ordained marriage.
Reflecting the Plan enduring through the ages
Commencing with the Marriage Supper of the Lamb.

Eden closed to your Heavenly Father's Heart of Heart.
Chosen My Creation Love to Cherish, Fellowship, and Protect.

Because I love you, My discipline must be invoked
Yet my love for you is everlasting.
My beloved to be conformed to the image of My Son.
My Love is faithful, pure, and true.

The wages of sin is death.
Spiritual death is separation from God, from your Heavenly Father.
From Jesus Christ The Lord and Savior
From the Holy Spirit who glorifies Jesus.
My love gift is eternal life available only through My Son Jesus
His Atoning Blood made provisional at the Cross.

Repent of your sin accepting forgiveness through the
Unblemished Lamb's Blood at Calvary.
Become co-heirs with Jesus
Through whom salvation alone is attained for Eternal Life.
Share His inheritance within
The Kingdom of God.

I have made the covenant provision through love sacrifice.

LOVE LETTERS FROM GOD
APPEAL FOR TRUTH

Dear Heart of My Heart
Do not despair midst your distress
The season of correction and discipline as it seems.
Troubles upon yourself overwhelmingly suppressive.
Allow your mind, your memory, your heart
To recall the sincerity of My Word of Truth.

Increase your faith as you believe My Word.
Persevere as your faith is tested
Refined as silver, and endurance is accomplished.
My Love remains constant.

Inquire of the Holy One who sustains your strength.
Seek wisdom and it is granted.
Prove Me says the Lord.
Holding abundant Life freely accessible to you
Mine alone and generously available.
The gift of Righteousness.

I implore you
Reign now in this life through Jesus My Son
As you will reign with Him throughout eternity.

Grasp firmly sound doctrine
Wavering not at the sound of deceiving misdirection.
Acknowledge Me. Recognize Me. Know Me.
Seek My Face.
Commit your aspiration to become Holy as I am Holy.
Your hope is in Truth.

As you acquire knowledge and understanding
Then as fully as I have known you
The mirror reflection's dimness will fade.
You will know Me as fully as you are known.

Love conquers all
Love is supremely abundant
Love is transcending every barrier.
Love is unending, and unfailing.
My Love is the path of Truth.

LOVE LETTERS FROM GOD
PROMISES

Dearly Beloved
My Promised One.

I am He who promised faithfulness
My Love will never leave you.
Return My Love as you live by faith in God The Father.
Believe My Holy Word.
You are made righteous in and through Jesus.

I will give you rest for your soul.
Take My yoke upon you. It is easy.
Learn from Me. I am gentle and humble in heart.

Dwell in the shelter of the Love of the Most High.
You shall abide, remain in the shadow of My Love and protection.
The very covering of the Almighty.
Seek the Lord and you will lack no good thing.
God is Love.

Life is precious to Me.
Love My Word, My precepts, the life I have lovingly given you.
Keep your speech, heart, and mind clean and acceptable.
You will see many good days
Enjoying every blessing within the realm of
My incomparable Love.

I your Lord am your portion.
I have assigned your cup, your lot,
I have established pleasant boundaries.

My Love provision is the beautiful, delightful, inheritance for you.

I remember My covenants.
My promises are true.
Delight in the Law of the Lord through meditation
Find prosperity in all you do.

These are My promises to you.

LOVE LETTERS FROM GOD
COMMITTED TO SLUMBERING ONE

Have you forsaken Me
Yet I will not release you.
My covenants are my commitment.
To the chosen, fashioned, promised, ordained, conforming
Adorned Bride of the Lord Jesus.

I honor My covenants to avenge you when wronged.
Protect you in danger.
Teach you through discipline.
Then sanctify you in due time with the hedge of thorns for protection
Against temptation removed
Time ensues to ministry season for edification.
Commitment reaches Glorification.

Reassurance I pronounce in your absence from
My fellowship presence.
I am patient. I am steadfast.
Within the expression of my everlasting Loving kindness
I establish our mutual love relationship and sin forgiveness.
Hold my promises true.
Salvation for Eternal Life through the provision of
My self-offering, sacrificial Son Jesus.

I have not wavered in My Loyalty
Though your wandering increases distance between us
I remain in all My truth-worthiness.

Your Committed Love.

LOVE LETTERS FROM GOD
EXPECTATIONS - HOPE

Dear Young Love
Expectation for creating My Companion
Purposing the delightful pleasure of enjoying the development of personal
Relationship.

My hope of the enduring Plan for the Love Origin from My Heart
Has never ceased for you to believe My Holy Word.

As you experience the death of a dream
Occasionally it may allow your conceiving My grief of disappointment
With the rejection of the hope I have so generously
Gifted Eden's family.

Likewise, the birth of a vision aids your visualizing the uplifting of
My Heart.
When Enoch accepted My hope and expectation
Thus, men began to call on The Name of The Lord.

The expectation for my chosen to return My Love
Have no other gods, Worship alone
The I Am
Soon rejected by all the legacy to worship.
Only Noah and his family saved for new hope.

Enoch with heart for God walked with Me three hundred years.
Fellowship pleasing the Heavenly Father.
Following generations departed from My Love.

The expectation of hope from My Heart constantly abides.

The certainty of my desire from your heart to unite with mine
Surely is incomprehensible.
My offering is your gift of desire to visualize your hope
Which is alone the Lord Jesus.

Oh, that your earnest hope and expectation
Ultimately reaches the summit pinnacle
That Christ is above all exalted.

Purposing the uniting of your hope and expectation
With the desire of your Holy God.

LOVE LETTERS FROM GOD
RESPONSE- MY DELIGHTFUL LOVE

Dear Bride Elect
You ask how shall I respond, order my days aright
Gain a heart of wisdom.

Acquire wisdom and understanding given
Do not turn away from My Word.
Fear God and keep My Commandments
Reverence the Holy Father Who Loves you.
Fear the Lord and receive understanding
Seek peace and pursue it, guarding your speech and avoiding evil.

Submission to molding as with the potters' wheel
Conformed to the image of My Son
Be transformed by the renewing of your mind.

Fulfill My Pleasure to bestow the desire of your heart.
Delight yourself in the Lord.
Trust in the Lord, depending upon Him
As the poor in Spirit
Finding success and establishment of your plans.

I know your intricate being.
You are more in value than the sparrow.
How beautiful is your love.

Search me that I may know my heart as clearly as I am known.

Pray in agreement with God without ceasing
Responding to the initiative of Holy God's desire and requirement.

For precious to God are man's thoughts
Likewise, the same as
From the Heart of the Holy Trinity.

My delightful Love.

LOVE LETTERS FROM GOD
LOVE OF MY HEART

I give you My Only Son Jesus.

Mine alone to give.
This gift offering valued at a greater price
Beyond Comprehension.

Past letters may seemingly appear vaguely mysterious
However, My Love for you expressed in numerous description
Encompasses Christ's Blood of the
Eternal Covenant.

My only Begotten Son
The Christ Child
The Messiah
Willingly sacrificed Himself
Even now as He shares in our sufferings
To satisfy the required penalty
For man's sin.

All who will may come, draw near
Accept salvation through the Atoning Blood
The unblemished sacrificial Lamb
Jesus Christ our Lord.

Receive the imparting of my assurance
The boundless Love I have for you.
Abide within the shelter of My Shadow
Reside midst the dwelling place of
The Most High.

The Word of God that you may know
With assurance My Incomprehensible Love for you

Love of My Heart.

LOVE LETTERS FROM GOD
A SPECIAL DELIVERY

You are mine. I have ransomed you.

I Want You
To respond to my love.
To place Holy God in your life's place, committed and assigned allegiance.
To know my love and the depth of my affection and concern
To accept the assurance of my unfailing love
All that comprises the essence of meaning.
To comprehend that I know you.
To accept that identity with you personally; Uniquely your individuality
As I designed, formed, developed, and ordained your birth.

I Want You
To prepare and provide a legacy, and inheritance for your children's children.
My Word I have given you.
The purity and Holiness of Truth.
The special gift shared with your loved ones.
My Holy Word residing in My Heart
Channeled through your heart
Imparted to your loving descendants
Circulating their hearts and lives to continue with their children
Until the Lord Jesus comes for His Bride, The Church.

I Have Plans For You
Plans that endure forever.

Walk With Me
Experience the presence of God.
Know love with your entire being.

Enjoy the intimate relationship and gain personal knowledge
Find greater depth of spirituality as you advance
In the same direction.
Accept the Truth of the Word of God.

Walk In My Ways
Seek and search for Me with confirmation I have loved you
Longer than you know.
Learn that My desire from the beginning established plan
Became your freedom of choice
To answer the divine call as one of My elect.
To commit your life to the obedience of My commandments
Requirements essential for Sanctification.
Walk even through interruption of displacement in absence of hope
Midst devastation, or apparent failure of accomplishments.

Walk In My Ways
Searching for Truth, seeking wisdom, learning The Face of the Lord
Committing the Word of God to memory in obedience of honor
Keep the Precepts to please the Savior,
Learning submissiveness and availability.
Loving the anticipation of Christ's appearing.
Know My Son Jesus to learn His many names,
To prepare for the Marriage Supper.

Walk With Me
To complete My Covenants
To Bless The Lord At All Times.

WHAT IS A NAME

The inner being of a personality
A person's reputation
A Banner to hold uprightly
To carry forth toward life's goals
Upheld, strengthened, and sustained
Reaching achievement and realizing victory.

Blessed is your name
Known by God our Heavenly Father from the beginning
Who has bestowed upon you the unique identity
All your very own inherited
Through your especially chosen parents
Each redeemed by the blood of the Lamb
Whose lives entwined in marriage ordained by God
Present the picture of Christ's love and commitment
To His Bride the Church.

Blessed is your name
For you are blessed creation of God's Love
Generous endowment gift from the Lord.

Blessed is your name
As you accept the enveloping love from each
Who surround you while we share God's love
And
Return the mystery in obedience to His Son
Jesus.

Circulating this unexplainable gift of love
Throughout our lives

We offer the sacrifice of praise.

Your Name is Wonderful.

Creation

The heavens are Thine, the earth also is Thine, the world and all it contains, Thou has founded them.

Psalm 89:11

Creation
Imagery View

The heavens are Thine, the earth also is Thine, the world and all it contains. Thou hast founded them.   Psalm 89:11

Let's Go See God

Craig and Elyse reach the height of their climb for the best viewing of the light show. Overhead and all around. They are awestruck by the light reflection of the shadows, and changing colors on the horizon.

Dusk, following early evening, escorts other events for display of creation. Beyond the foothills, mountain peaks reach to magnify the Creator. The trees stand tall to lift their boughs in praise.

Nearby the waterways sound as one voice to meet and join the majestic seas. While the mighty waters roll, swelling waves touch the shore with promise to return.

Twilight fades deferring to a crystal clear sky, and welcoming the rising moon. The day of creation experience approaches closure.

The children's optional choice to closing is, "Let's go see God."

Worship of God
Displayed

CREATION

Consider Word Of God	Ecclesiastes 7:13
Jesus Finished God's Work	John 4:34
Creation In Him All Things Created	Colossians 1:16
MAGNIFICENT MASTER PLAN	Romans 8:17, 29
WORK OF SPLENDOR	2 Corinthians 5:21
CHERISHED LEGACY PROMISED	Romans 8:29
AN EXCELLENT WIFE	Proverbs 12:4

MAGNIFICENT MASTER PLAN

God's gifts to me I cannot count them easily.
Life following formation
Then the provision of eternal life, Salvation and Forgiveness.
Through the plan divinely ordained in Jesus His Son,
Becoming God Incarnate.

With continuous expression of His Love
I know Mercy, Grace, Blessings.
Granting the immeasurable audience and presence within the realm
Of gifts to behold in the plan of the
Priesthood of the Believer.

Becoming one of many known from the beginning
Enjoined with the family of God
Now amazed to receive the joint heir-ship
With Christ
Mine to claim as rightful owner.

Family, husband, children, grandchildren,
Fellowship and Friendship, I can hardly this joy contain
Not to be compared with the assurance of security
Bestowed with Sealing of the Holy Spirit.

The Gifts of the Spirit
Acquired through the knowledge, wisdom, and understanding
From Spiritual insight gained within
Love from the Word of God.

Holding firmly to our gift of hope
Anticipating the miraculous eternal life legacy

Love for each other is attained.
The gifts of ministry find place of service
As we appropriate the
Power of the Holy Spirit.

Our Heavenly Father
In His indescribable generosity
Continues dispersing delightful blessing gifts daily.
Many not recognized are the
Ordained steps and path direction provided
Through every good and perfect gift
From above.

Not least of which is the free will and choice
Included in the Master Plan from
The Heart of God
Giving His Only Begotten Son
Allowing the Crown of Righteousness.

WORK OF SPLENDOR

May you see the beautiful blossoms adorning the trees
And garden fair.
Feel now the lovely summer breeze
That cools the air
Refreshes the soul abundantly.

Allow this time the sun's warmth to melt your fears
Embrace your heart and encourage your hope for strength.
Sing praise and give thanks
To our Heavenly Father for each new day of life
For the love of family and friends.
In joyful gratitude grasp the experience of the
Creation of earth's beauty.

Sensing the intangible blessings
Imparted as realistically as one knows the touch of a loved one
Enjoy every good and perfect gift which comes from above.
Accept the incomparable love of Holy God
Being comforted within the security and assurance
Found only in Jesus our Lord.

Season for contemplation and moments of reflection
Now appear beckoning attention for time to encompass the need for
Quiet, peaceful, serenity.

The graciousness of our Heavenly Father surrounds His loved ones.
Abides within the shadow of concern and protective plan
The unending endurance of God's purpose completed
Encircles our life as a stream flows toward
The intersection to become an integral part of nature's balance.

Visionaries bring understanding that
Our Holy God is Love.
Love that transcends our comprehension.
Yet the Love we know which God the Father originates
Channels through His Only Begotten Son Jesus
Circulating through your heart and my heart
For our sharing with each other.
Creation's work of grandeur is expressed through the artistic gift
God's Own Work.

CHERISHED LEGACY PROMISED

A Son Was Promised. A Son Was Given.
He The Only Heir To The Throne Of Heaven.
A Promise is a Promise to be fulfilled. And it was so.
Through the Son's absence in Heaven was ordained by The Father
While Our Lord visited Earth.
Yet the Planned Purpose indwelling Jesus as He grew
Found Him in favor with God
And He continued growing in Obedience.

As the Rainbow colors blend
Many are the promises we are given
Only to receive to become co-heirs with Christ.

How majestically beautiful
This rainbow of colors in the sky to be seen and shared by all.
The exquisite profusion distinctly expressing hope's beginning
Ending as designed to capture the awesome work of creation,
Promise, and Purpose for man to know the expanse of God's Love.

God's Vow is everlasting as the Rainbow
Constant in shape, design, and color.

Jesus is the Rock of our Salvation
His Word is pure as
The Rainbow is like no other.

AN EXCELLENT WIFE

From the beginning when the Word was with God
The Word was God
Man and Wife were magnificently designed
Eminently original from
The Heart of The Lord God.

Man's good established finding his wife
The extension presented
Awaiting only the spiritual completion
As husband and wife becoming
Joint-heirs with Christ
Joining The Kingdom Of God.

Two now sharing equal position of
Submissiveness, Love, and Respect
Acknowledging the authority
From The Godhead.

Man assigned responsibility as leader
Within the family and home.
Cleaving to his wife, leaving other family emotionally
While obediently and respectively
Honoring Parents, Grandparents
And
All ordained legacy of inheritance.

Truly man is crowned with
God's Gift of
An Excellent Wife.

Life

In Thy right hand there are pleasures forever. For with Thee there is the fountain of life.

Psalm 16:11c, Psalm 36:9a

Life
Imagery View

Within the diligent quest for security, we have come to know the awesome wonder of God's purpose. The splendor of creation, complete for all enduring time, remains at rest in God's good works throughout the universe. The sixth day's closing gives credence to history.

The Lord God proclaimed, "Let us make man in our image."

Prefacing the purpose for the precious gift of life for man, the Word with God perceived the plan that was established from the foundation of the world. That life is the gift from God, for God is love.

Foreknowing the need of man, within His own desire for the abundant life, God arranged for man's provisions. He fashioned woman from Adam's rib, then presented her to him for his wife.

The steppingstone Path of Life is made known to man. The Stones are significant as each step along the Journey leads toward Eternal Assurance.

Path of Life
Journey

LIFE

Life Gift Of Love	Genesis 2:7
Man's Honor Bestowed	Genesis 9:6
Make Man Our Image	Genesis 1:27
Glory To God	1 Corinthians 11:2
Invisible God	Colossians 1:15

Life   Standard of Life According To Thy Word   Psalm 119:9

CONSECRATED WITH PURPOSE   Lamentations 2:17

HEAVENLY DESIGN LIFE UNIQUE   Psalm 16:5, Psalm 133:1-3

THAT I MIGHT HAVE LIFE   Proverbs 8:35, Psalm 103:4

THE BEAUTY OF LIFE   John 3:16, Psalm 48:2

MOTHER

STEPPINGSTONES   Psalm 16:11, Psalm 119:133

CONSECRATED WITH PURPOSE

Known before design, formation, and loved before the beginning of time
Created uniquely like no other
Self standing, alone.

Placed in family divinely ordained surrounded by care and others
Identity assumed though inheritance
Consecrated and established aright only to know the essence of love's
Meaning fully matured.

Insignificant streaming blonde shadow, poor, sad, and unsmiling,
Frequent hesitancy enjoined by fear of rejection
The occasions of acceptance found encouragement rekindled.
Lifted from depths of despair, indignity of poverty felt
Within the appearing shadows
Slowly the directed light led toward hope.

Then more beautiful than Queen Esther's lovely story
United heart and spirit.
Human will respond to an inaudible call, thus another beginning.
Grace experienced, yet unrecognized, Love transcended, endless,
Unceasing, Eternally Sealed.

Single, yet between two brothers,
Each playing, music, exploring, collecting experiences as a single child
Blending, mingling, nevertheless continuously interchangeable,
Remaining separate personalities bonding supportiveness developed.

Abruptly separated through the pangs of heartbreak
Once again joined within loss and need only to find divisible lonely paths
Two in different places.

Then as sunshine escapes the clouds so long a familiar companion
Brother home returning.
School days together a season to cherish, unaware of time to relish,
All too soon another period disappearing.
Absence and dis-joining now abandons someone else alone.

Childhood sharing almost lost
God's working together for good severed path intersected
For purpose of later pleasant fulfillment wonder.

As days and years span distance, our family realizes resumed closeness
Separate homes occupied yet sharing holidays and other
Visits more frequently
Affords greater enhancement to faded love in grief and suffering.

My lot, my portion assigned
The boundaries of my life became pleasant places within God's purpose.
Inheritance delightfully promised.

Exuberant happiness, a sweet uniting combination of wonder,
And astonishment adjustment to these awesome miracles,
Miracles whose heart melting grasp
Permanently take hold never to be replaced by
Any other gift.
The innocence of children.
This invasion of routine existence accelerates the pace of progress
Toward growth and spiritual maturity.

Time to continue along life's course
Advancing crossroads, and darkened distance
Often bring doubt with confusion
Until Faith in God's Word see steps and choices directed.

Blessings showing abundant growth
Pain of change interrupts with harsh awareness.
Soul confronts conscience
Temptation subsides
Obedience is Victory!

Knowledge visits
Precept is entertained
Meditative Prayer becomes practice
Life envelopes insight and make preparation for testimonies.

New interests surfacing focus appears in different forms.
Remain my heart within the shelter
Secure in the abiding overshadowing of the Almighty
The Most High.

Waves of apprehension, overwhelming fear,
Persistent storms of hesitancy to believe.
Silent desire of reassurance restored.
God is in control.
Wounded and exhausted spirit finds sustaining strength.

Feeling alone, abandoned, rejected,
The Cross envisioned renews motivation
Allowing the privilege of sharing Christ's sufferings
Bringing His Plan and Purpose to completion.

Where is this place?
Unlike a previous recognition
Very Strange.
Engulfed in past panic recollection
Facing social hostility

Consuming tightening constraint
Like the swallowing recurrence of homesickness. Where?
Day, Night, light, Insight.
God Is Here!

Where?
Here.
God is Near.
Stance resumed as supportive Sustainer constantly remains.

Yes! A new place of renewed commitment
To follow the Light along the path of life straight ahead.
Reassurance illuminating each carefully led step
Following the Light of the World
Jesus.

Conviction meets opposition
Other points of view compel search seeking wisdom
Receiving requires understanding.
The Holy Spirit explains meaning
Holy Scripture confirms thoughts, logics, questions.
Heart searching satisfies quest.
Trust in the Lord.

Gratitude offering for each New Day of Life.
Expected turmoil returns, returns, returns.
Repetitious Faith translates Hope.

Another gracious blessing from God
One within so many
Receiving the petitioned wisdom and understanding
For each instance to know Jesus' example

In making every decision pleasing the Lord.

Overwhelming deceptive need for fulfillment
Seemingly consumes my attention
To be first in a husband's life
To enjoy error of perspective pleasantries for personalities
Consideration material and temporal gain.

Acquired assurance of peaceful heart
Should temptation present the choice
I will with unwavering gratitude and consecrated commitment renewed
Thank my Heavenly Father for His continuous bequest
Upon my humble reception of the
Divine Word Phrases
To impart to those God answers prayer for encouragement
To inspire and motivate to accept
His gifts of Measure of Faith, and to actively increase personal faith.

I also accept this Poetic Gift
Rather experience the absence of personal communion
With Holy God
As He reveals Jesus' many aspects of Grace
In lieu of earthly companionship.

In reply to Our Heavenly Father's bidding
My humble heart follows
Walk With Me.

HEAVENLY DESIGN LIFE UNIQUE

Golden phases enter, intervening,
Time appearing mundane, meaningless.
Recall forthcoming gives precedence plaguing rejection.
Renewed awakened confidence
Render anticipating strides toward progressing distant sites to attain.

Abiding connection entwined in sight
Hence faithfulness of Holiness seizes faltering semblance of thwarted
Misinterpretation.
Meaningless circumstances frequently questioned, found maimed.
Moments cherished extend throughout experiences gleaned as
Integral reaping harmonious, peaceful accord.
Visualizing Spiritual Purpose The Living Word becomes Revealed.

Day to Day routine of moving through life enraptured the soul.
One may term experiences.
Evolving assurance strengthens faith, believing the Word becomes alive.
Revealing our assigned lot, portion, cup, beneficial blessings.
Triumphantly thrusting forward
Victory within circumstances.

Glorious is the fresh perception to reflect Christ.
Sobering is the realization
Warfare is at hand threading its existence throughout our
Life's weaving pattern
Introducing the Fruit of The Spirit potential encompassed by the
Protective armor.
Oh! Such a design is the Heavenly Intent
A personal, unlike another, plan completed
To present to Jesus Our Lord.

My prayer to embrace my gift of heart's desire
Within the loom assigned.
To allow this intricate work uninterrupted
Faith replacing doubt, destroying disobedience,
Contentment recognizing pleasant boundaries.
Following the order of direction to meet my Creator With a
Heart of Wisdom.
The fabric of my life acceptable
Conformed to The Image of Christ.

Experiences unattained subside, diminishing growth,
Passivity prevailing.
Buds of spring nurtured emit development
Bursting forth in full blossom.
Likewise one's acceptance to incidental events
Evokes the concurrence to God's fashioning a single life
His unique creation.

THAT I MIGHT HAVE LIFE

So many preceding this space I now occupy ordained by our
Heavenly Father
To establish the line of heritage, my ancestors, my parents,
Planned in the scheme of creation
Each designed in a unique individual known before conception
Holiness origin of the Trinity held before beginning of Time.

Oh! That my name was spoken within Eternity's Plan
Awaiting only passing seasons to experience the purposeful birth
Delivered and presented to this world assigned as companion
For Obedience to please The Creator.

Our sovereign God preserved the lives of men, soldiers of war
In ancient combat,
Our country's civil battles, Pearl Harbor.
Women surviving disease, difficult years of growing,
Sharing family responsibility,
Learning Christian standards of living at early ages,
Children allowed to escape disappointment in their tender lives,
Frequently spirits wounded,
Harmful disaster averted to reach adulthood to continue
The Family Tree.
That I Might Live!

That my children, their spouses, my grandchildren, my husband
Might live.
Encompassing Our Lord's foreknowledge
My Eternal Security is sealed.
I know Jesus Christ as personal Savior.
His salvation provision, The Atoning Blood at Calvary grants I am

Coheirs with Him
Through my repentance and Redemption found only in
Gifts of Freedom of Grace.

Paths of life revealed as paths made straight and narrow
Accompanying the gracious Path of Peace.
All God's work freely given for all designed that none remain lost.

Gratefully, and humbly I offer my Praise To God The Father
For Giving His Only Son Jesus.
God The Son who willingly in obedience paid for sins for
All mankind.
Crucifixion, Death, Burial, Resurrection,
To ascend To God The Father.

Jesus Lives!
Accomplished Companionship With The Holy Trinity
Throughout Unending Eternity
Now in time absorbing the pleasures of gifts and blessings
The Abundant Life
Then bowing in worshipful adoration
Continuing to acknowledge all The Creator's Work
That I Might Have Life!

THE BEAUTY OF LIFE

Oh! To pen the visionaries of God's Gifts.
The awesome creation and splendor of Nature's Beauty
How marvelously gifted with life at Birth's Appearance.
The ordained Purpose Provision of Eternal Presence
Worshiping Jesus our Lord and Savior.

Behold the significance through God-given senses.
Sight experienced considering the universe,
Earth's Landscapes, Seascapes, Mountain Ranges, Rainbows,
Sunsets, Sunrise, A New Day of Life, Christmas Celebration,
Miraculous newborn babies, the lovely Body of Believers
Harken to celestial sounds of music only God can orchestrate
Taste the satisfying quest for Righteousness obtained in salvation.

Touch the intangible truth of the incomparable Love at the
Redemptive Calvary Cross.
Relish the fragrant gardens of Jesus' Names, sweetest above all others.
Lily of the Valley, Rose of Sharon.

The Beauty of Life circulates from God's Heart
Through hours sharing His Love.

Life's most Beautiful Blessing Never Ceasing
New Life in Christ through His Atoning Blood.
The Beauty of Life
Extending Throughout Eternity.

MOTHER

One of the dearest treasures held within our heart of hearts
Second only to our Savior
Jesus Our Lord.
God's first gift in life
Mother.

Our Heavenly Father's omnipotent family design
Ordained legacy provision of parent heritage
Blessed our lives with the nurturing, caring, and loving we have known
Especially in the Mother's role.

Within Mother's ministry of service
She achieved making successful our aspirations, life's goals and
Realization of our hopes and dreams.

It is with humble gratitude we offer our tribute
In praise to Holy God
To honor Mother for her life and love as she remains in our hearts
And her memory continues in our children and her grandchildren.

Among God's many gifts bestowed freely through His grace
We recall Mother and visionaries
Appear repeatedly in nature's beauty.
Within the sound of music.
Acknowledging the glory of sunset from the ocean's shore.
Viewing the awesome snow capped mountains.
The purity of beholding a new born baby.

We cannot forget the encouragement
The understanding we've experienced during time of disappointment.

Not the least of which
Mother contributed toward the molding and conforming
Children's character and likeness
To become perfected in the Image of Christ.

May the Holy Spirit continue to
Gain control in our lives
As we learn Jesus' desire to please the Holy Father in submissiveness
And
We glean the blessings known before
Expressed through patience, diligence, wisdom, and faith of Mother.

STEPPINGSTONES

Discernment accompanies the quest for wisdom
Truth of the Scripture confirms the request
For understanding is imparted.
Oh! How could there have been confusion
Permeating the mind
In opposition to the consecrated heart.
In retrospect it is amazing questions surfacing
As recall summons time past of imposing weight
Bearing down upon the soul.
Then clarity of contemplation assuredly envisioned
The Holy Plan.
Searching began to identify the mission, assigned service
Progressive moments aligned
Combating the unsightly head of intrusion that rose
Against the trusting soul.
Weariness waned with passage of season.
Allowing new perspective and focus
Upon the lighted path ordained for continuing
The walk along the steps others have trod.
Engulfing heaviness disappears
Taking Jesus' Yoke He offers as the easy bundle to carry
Welcoming the shared prevailing responsibility
Accompanying Sharing Christ's Sufferings.
As two move along the same direction.
Learning, sharing, within
Holy Communion.
The journey leads toward preparation for future growth
The tapestry of life is interwoven
As the ministry thread finds strong attachment with other
Stitches previously sewn.

Know assuredly prayer is supportive
Just as surely as the stones of faith are grounded
In the Lovely Cornerstone
Sufficient for any measure of weight.

Covenant

¹⁰*All the paths of the Lord are loving-kindness and truth to those who keep His covenant and His testimonies.* ¹⁴*The secret of the Lord is for those who fear Him, and He will make His covenant known.*

Psalm 25:10, 14

The New Covenant Cup
Imagery View

The agreement promise of God's covenant will never be forsaken. He ordained the Covenant-Inheritance, and it is established not to be abandoned.

For the scripture to be fulfilled, Jesus revealed, the cup of the covenant is for Jesus' blood, which the Father has given to Me. The New Covenant Cup is poured out in My blood.

Jesus' blood on His cross, poured out for salvation, is the cup of the Eternal Covenant, who is the Christ. For God in the blood of Jesus, brought up from the dead the Great Shepherd, who is the Eternal Covenant, Jesus.

The cup of submission to the Father's will. The servant, as a ransom for many offered Himself unblemished to God, and a sacrificial offering of His blood on His cross made peace.
Reconciling all things to Himself. Remaining the covenant cup of submission in obedience to the will of God the Eternal Father.

The Lord's lovingkindness is everything to everlasting on those who fear Him, who keeps His covenant.

Psalm 103:17a, 18a (paraphrased)

The New Covenant
Cup Of My Blood

COVENANT

Companionship	Genesis 1:26
Ordained Family	Genesis 2:18
Noah Walked With God	Genesis 6:9
In Abram All Families Of Earth Blessed	Acts 3:25
Covenant	Psalm 25:10

COVENANT TRILOGY
And God Ordained His Covenant   Psalm 111:9

    FAMILY   Man, Helper, Woman, Children   Genesis 2:18,22
Genesis 4:1

    BLESS THIS HOUSE
        Fellow Citizens Are Of God's Household   Ephesians 2:19

    HOME   God Has Established His Throne
       In Heavens   Psalm 103:19

NEW COVENANT
    Jesus Guarantee Better Covenant   Hebrew 7:22

CHRISTMAS
    A Son Was Promised A Son Was Given   John 1:23

PURSUE PEACE
    The God Of Peace Raised From The Dead
    The Great Shepherd Through the Blood Of The
    Eternal Covenant Even Jesus Our Lord   Hebrews 13:20

Christ Is Our Peace   Ephesians 2:14

COVENANT TRILOGY
FAMILY

The Heavenly Father's plan
For each individual
Designed birth, life, journey path
Ordained to please
The Creator.

God's gracious gifts comprise
The Family Home.

Offering praise for compassion
Experiencing love, gratitude, grace
Bless The Lord's Name.

The purpose in His timing
Magnifies Jesus' Sacrifice
Through peace in His Blood
For our redemption
On His Cross.

Completing the line of Legacy
Family branches extend
From our tree
To Eternal Security.

Within The Church Family
Exalting God's Name Together
Ceaselessly One Family.

COVENANT TRILOGY
BLESS THIS HOUSE

Bless This House Oh Lord We Pray.

We Offer To You Praise In Thanksgiving,
For Every Family, For Each Home
Represented. For other Members
Comprising Our Family House.
We gather To Thank You For Providing
Our Daily Bread Needs, Our Food,
Our Time In Your Purpose To Love
Each Other As We Break Bread
Together.

The Holy Spirit In His Temple
Praise God In His Place, Who
Causes our House To Stand And
To Remain Undivided. Open To
All Who Will Know Our Welcome
Invitation.
Thank You For Our House Of The
United States Of America.
We Pray For Healing And Unity.

In Jesus' Name We Rejoice. We
Will Join The Heavenly Host In
The Prepared House Of
Mansions, To Dwell Throughout
Eternity.

AMEN

COVENANT TRILOGY
HOME

There! Lights are enhanced by starlight
Trimmed tree reflecting Jesus' first cradle
For the light of the World.

Anticipation for family visit intensifies
Approaching homes to celebrate Christmas.
Bethlehem House of David
The Christ Child's home open to receive
Love gifts of worship
Thus our family house welcomes all who enter.

Sublime emotions indwell each
Enveloping home atmosphere.

Pleasure permeates the recalling visions
Presently collecting and joining new ones
To sustain the warmth of
Family Home
Time flees midst love ones' farewell
Heartfelt emptiness with you replenished.
Parted from earthly dwelling
Yet Praise to Holy God has only begun.

Jesus Lives
The elect, The Church gather reunited
Praise Together
Worship Forever

Home

NEW COVENANT

One God One Mediator between God and men
Jesus the mediator of New Covenant

Magnificent gift of love In My Blood
God brought up from the dead Jesus
Mediator through the Blood of the eternal covenant.

Jesus the mediator guarantee of a better covenant
Summons lovingly Come To Me
Hear Me and listen that you may live
And I will make an everlasting covenant with you.

God made us adequate as servants
Of a New Covenant
Thine space of the spirit who gives life.
Offering to God submitting without blemish
I pour out this cup for you
The new Covenant in my Blood.
For this reason Christ is the mediator
Of a new Covenant through the eternal spirit.

He tasted death for everyone's redemption.
Those who are called may receive
The promise of the eternal inheritance
Reconciling all things to himself
Through the Blood of His cross.

Jesus covenant of promise established Peace.
Christ is our peace fulfilled are words of prophets,
Ruler comes from Bethlehem who will

Shepherd My people Israel.
Offspring of David and Bethlehem.
Glory to God Peace among men.

Lord's loving kindness from generation to generation
To those who keep His covenant and remember to do them.

CHRISTMAS
Celebration With Family And Friends

The seasons of joy, love and giving, similar to that
First clear starlight night
The Birth of God's Son Jesus
The ultimate gift of magnitude from our Heavenly Father.

CHRISTMAS

A snowy white wonderland with joyful sounds of music filling the air
Visions of a snow covered stable surrounded by heralding angels
Offering Glory To God For The Christ Child

CHRISTMAS

A time the heart turns homeward with thoughts of lights,
Decorated trees, exchanging gifts, sharing holiday visits
Echoing the Nativity Scene
A tree became a cradle, another a cross.
The brightest star positioned within a pattern of divine order
Guided the shepherds then the wise men from the east
To reach the Adorning Child
Who would become the good shepherd.
Leading lost sheep to become found among the eternally secure.
There lying in a manger
Wrapped in cloths purposed for preparation for death, burial,
Resurrection
Our Savior's presentation made the essential provision
For our following and reaching
The gloriously prepared Heavenly Home.
Absence of separation, Eternal presence with our Lord Jesus.
Once the baby born in Bethlehem.

CHRISTMAS

Fulfillment for the soul and glowing enthrallment for the heart.
The most wonderful event for celebration
In man's history for a man's future.

HAPPY BLESSED CHRISTMAS

PURSUE PEACE

There in the distant shadow space beyond comprehension
Asserting recognition, a glimpse becoming more distinctively in focus
Peace.
Each seeking this solace of life, searching for the comforting assurance
Known alone within the enveloping cocoon provisional of
Meaningful security.
The peace of mind translates tranquility extending
Beyond understanding.
Man's quest, appeal, endeavor, to experience the inner calming
Grace reaching the soul's serenity
Discovered in Christ Jesus Our Lord.

Pursue Peace, finding its presence, accepting the God gifted Joy,
The evolving love within this sphere of the original purpose to unite
The perfect relationship
Among the Creator and all mankind the foundation of God's pleasure.

Seek this universal hope, the abundant life, the wound of healing,
Elegant, achievement of Freedom.
A single person's prayerful desired peaceful soul and spirit
Begins the circulation of far reaching reconciliation essential for
Completing the harmony
Encircling the world, fulfillment the Divine Design,
Ordained before the beginning of time.

As the universe was set in place, creation through the Word of God,
Was spoken into existence.
He proclaimed, "Let there be peace on earth."
His peace, A Gift Of Love,
For the Brotherhood of all people.

Legacy

⁵*Predestined to be adopted as sons through Jesus Christ to Himself according to God's purpose, ^{11a}we have obtained an inheritance.*
¹³*Delivered us from the domain of darkness, and transferred to the kingdom of His beloved Son. ³⁴Those on His right will hear the King say, "Come, inherit the kingdom prepared for you from the foundation of the world."*

Ephesians 1:5, 11a; Colossians 1:13; Matthew 5:34 (paraphrased)

Legacy Kingdom Castle
Imagery View

The Legacy Purpose to prepare for the most beautiful Inheritance reveals God's promise. His Inheritance never forsaken, nor the promise abandoned. In God's graciousness, the born again is predestined to obtain His Inheritance that is imperishable. Eternal life with the Lord Jesus.

Preparation's segment of the Legacy- Inheritance extends and encompasses all who are the heirs of God. As we are children of God, we are heirs of God. We are fellow-heirs of Christ.

Our Inheritance is chosen for us, for the Lord Most High is a great King over all the earth. He predestined that we obtain an inheritance according to His purpose, who works all things after the counsel of His will.

Inherit the Prepared Kingdom

LEGACY

Eternity Ownership
Purposed Legacy   Hebrews 6:17

God's Purpose Predestined
We Obtain An Inheritance   Ephesians 1:11

Chosen Before Foundation
Of The World   Ephesians 1:4

Lord Not Abandon Or Forsake His Inheritance   Psalm 94:14

Legacy   Ordained Gift   Genesis 9:8-9

HONOR YOUR PARENTS
GOD'S GIFT AND LEGACY   Exodus 20:12

LIGHTHOUSE
Sounding Call Direction   Ephesians 1:18

A RAINBOW OF PROMISES
Eternal Life-Joint-Heir   Matthew 19:29

HONOR YOUR PARENTS
GOD'S GIFT AND LEGACY

In humble adoration I offer my praise of thanksgiving
To our Heavenly Father
Who reveals the mystery of His love
In part with the gift of His understanding.

The purpose of creation within the eternal plan
Ordained to give form and birth to each uniquely chosen child of God
Designed for His pleasure of companionship
His desire for likewise responsive love.

The love of God supremely extended
Toward His distinguished affectionate one
Surpasses all comprehension of the encompassing value and regard
Held in Holy Heart for
His esteemed elect.

One of the divine gifts so perfectly ordained
We received as inheritance
Through the chartered line of ancestors
Discovered within the
Depth of God the Father's Covenant Promise
Our Parents.

We love Holy God
Because He first loved us.
We love our earthly father because
God has directed our love, respect, and honor
To be given to His commandments for obedience

To know He has selected and presented personally
To each of us the perfectly designed
And
Ordained father within the predetermined
Line of ancestry.

LIGHTHOUSE

As pain and sorrow persist, seemingly to remain,
Darkness pervades surrounding each change
In a new position
Difference in scenery or sanctuary for prayer.

Then hope's shadow flows over as a comforting cloud
To shelter from the all too heat of intensity.

One hears the song of a bird,
The Wind,
The Quiet.

Solace moves across and the feeling occurs as waves wash the shore
Returning to sea, and returning again,
And once more.

Oh! How peaceful the soul becomes
Flowing into time for moments of tranquility
Inspiring a season of praise and heartfelt joy.
That exaltation of the inward being.

Discomfort may occur with less intensity.
The hope of renewal gives meaning to the heart for strengthened faith.

Belief in God's Word of always being with you
Never forsaking His Loved Ones.
The Lighthouse
Always escorting your hope change direction,
Turning and following Jesus
Wherever He Leads.

115

A RAINBOW OF PROMISES

A Son Was Promised. A Son Was Given.
He The Only Heir To The Throne Of Heaven.

A Promise is a Promise to be fulfilled. And it was so.
Through the Son's absence in Heaven was ordained by the Father
While Our Lord visited Earth.
Yet the planned Purpose indwelling Jesus as He grew
Found Him in favor with God
And He continued growing in Obedience.

As the Rainbow colors blend
Many are the promises we are given
Only to receive to become co-heirs with Christ.

How majestically beautiful
This rainbow of colors in the sky to be seen and shared by all.
The exquisite profusion distinctly expressing hope's beginning
Ending as designed to capture the awesome work of creation,
Promise, and purpose for man to know the expanse of God's Love.

God's Vow is everlasting as the Rainbow
Constant in shape, design and color.

Jesus is the Rock of our Salvation
His Word is pure as
The Rainbow is like no other.

Gifts

Within His purposed plan, God's gift generously bestowed, accomplish the desire of His wondrous pleasure presenting the redeemed the free gift of God, eternal life.

Based on Romans 3:24

Gifts Of Grace & Love
Imagery View

I show you a more excellent way to earnestly desire the greater gifts of ministry. Walk in love as Christ also loved you and gave Himself for us.

Love one another for love is from God. He so loved the life of everyone in mankind's creation that He gave His only Son to pay our sin debt. Through Jesus' death and blood on His cross, we have eternal life.

As we exercise the gifts given in grace for ministry we serve in love. We walk in love giving a cup of water cold, and food to those who hunger.

Love walks a second mile to help a stranger in need. A traveler from afar, robbed and left for dead, was ignored by two men of their prominent community. A journeyman passing through the same area bandaged the helpless man, used his own transportation to find assistance for the injured. Paying the cost of service, the Samaritan promised to return and reimburse the care giver for added expense.

Love is giving time, resources and hope. Love is kindness, expressed in compassions; joy in the Lord expresses Love.

Ultimate Gift
of Love

GIFTS

God's Only Son   God So Loved The World   John 3:16

Grace   My Grace Is Sufficient For You   2 Corinthians 12:9
         Opposed To Proud Grace To Humble   James 4:6

Children   A Gift Of The Lord   Psalm 127:3

Gifts   Every Perfect Gift From Heaven Above   James 1:17

MY PRAISE RESPONSE
         The Heavens Praise Thy Wonders   Psalm 89:5

MOTHERS
         Commandment Honor Mother   Deuteronomy 5:16
         Man Named Wife Eve Mother All Living   Genesis 3:20
         Honor Mother That Your Days Are Prolonged   Exodus 20:12

LOVE RETURNED

GOD'S GIFT OF FRIENDSHIP
         Loves At All Times   Proverbs 17:17

ONE SPECIAL GIFT   Motivation To Please God   1 Peter 4:10

MY PRAISE RESPONSE

To please Him the purpose
For my being created.
An invitation to know the
Lord's Requirements.

To love the Lord your God
With all your heart, soul, and might.
Obedience following.
In desire to keep the commandments.
Reverence for the written Scripture
And
Gratitude offerings presented
In praise and song.
Love your neighbor as yourself.

Discover acceptable behavior
And
The maturing faith gleaned from
Works accountable refined by
Purification and awarded as crowns to be
Laid at Jesus' feet
At the judgment Seat of Christ.
My ultimate gift to God.

I dedicate all that I possess
With the response of stewardship
Returning to God all rights of ownership
Which He has so generously
Showered upon me.

My gift of gratitude I offer
For the divine protection
Held within His provision available to me
For everything entrusted in my care.

Through creative self-expression
I lift my heart in tribute.
To God Be All The Honor And Glory.

His innumerable gifts including
The gift of self-expression
So unique, yet very familiar
Prompt my response.

Commitment to obedience
And gratitude present
My reply to the revealed
Proposed plan for completion.
That which conforms
To the image of Christ.

MOTHERS

One of the dearest treasures held within our heart of hearts
Second only to our Savior Jesus our Lord.
God's first gift in life
Mother.

Our Heavenly Father's omnipotent family design
Ordained legacy provision of parent heritage
Blessed our lives with the nurturing, caring, and loving we have known
Especially in the Mother's roll.

Within Mother's ministry of service
She achieved making successful our aspirations, life's goal and
Realization of our hopes and dreams.

It is with humble gratitude we offer our tribute
In praise to Holy God
To honor Mother for her life and love as she remains in our hearts
And her memory continues in our children and her grandchildren.

Among God's many gifts bestowed freely through His grace
We recall Mother and visionaries
Appear repeatedly in nature's beauty.
Within the sound of music.
Acknowledging the glory of sunset from the ocean's shore
Viewing the awesome snow capped mountains.
The purity of beholding a new born baby.

We cannot forget the encouragement
The understanding we've experienced during time of disappointment.
Not the least of which

Mother contributed toward molding and conforming her
Children's character and likeness
To become perfected in the image of Christ.

May the Holy Spirit continue to
Gain control in our lives
As we learned Jesus' desire to please the Holy Father in submissiveness
And
We glean the blessing known before
Expressed through patience, diligence, wisdom and faith of
MOTHER.

LOVE RETURNED
GOD'S GIFT OF FRIENDSHIP

Agape' Love superlative to the imagination
The encompassing grandeur of
Glorious Beauty within the Universal Sphere.

The incomparable, unconditional, filled with
Grace, freedom, selflessness, and generosity,
God's Love.

No requirement expectation of sacrifice to receive.
Yet our Lord's desire is our obedience
To attain His bountiful Life established
And Plan of Provision.

Love the Lord your God with all your heart, mind, strength.
Where is there space to find for another's love
Love for our children, spouse, friend.

How precious is that plan of origin.
The Creation, Salvation, atonement, reconciliation
The love of God.
Christ's sacrificial Love.
The assigned area of the soul, mind, will, and emotion,
For returning His Love.
Throughout that exceptional bequest of friendship.

Loving God
Returned capacity for
Loving each other.

ONE SPECIAL GIFT

Eleven years of age, and God's call is clearly heartfelt.
Come follow Me, for I am Truth.
The gift of my Lord's desire that He is Love and Purpose for my life
Becoming indwelling to respond
In obedience to please Him.

Before my Beginning
The Holy Father's provision ceases not.
Humanistic need developed assertion
Choices wisely and poorly assume shaping personality
Following direction necessitated God intended intervention.

Remaining constant are the scales of life
God is in control
Man has free will.
There is purpose in God's timing
His plan ultimately reaches completion.

I chose my husband, yet He pursued my interest.
This the celestial mutual marital ministry established.
We also serve as we stand beside, become available,
And support in prayer.

Two in love, unaware of underlying need, or requirements, or barriers.
Spiritual growth reveals past unidentified surfacing truth
Allowing insight recognition.

My lot, My Lord's portion, my cup
Transpires to assignment of life's unique place of pleasant boundaries.
Personally created purpose to find fulfillment in the generous

Bequests from God
Salvation, husband, home, children, and grandchildren.
Other ministries, a sum of conformity to Christ's image.

My special gift bestowed to motivate my every decision to pleasing
The Heavenly Father
Initiates every action toward proclaiming
Truth
Jesus The Messiah.

The continuous ministry remains as first imparted from the
Imploring vow until death parted.
Other ministries offer presentations within the Holy Spirit's timing.
Another is encouraged.
I am blessed abundantly over.

Ministry

Ministry is given within varying periods of life's journey to fulfill the purpose of Christ's more excellent ministry in love.

Based on Hebrews 8:6 & 1 Corinthians 12:5-7

Ministry
Imagery View

Whatever you do in My name, you have done it unto Me.

To fulfill the purpose of the more excellent ministry is to love one another.

The beautiful church building marks the center of the town as a pearl beacon glistens in the sunlight. The steeple rising toward the heavens supports the cross of gold, proclaiming Jesus is Lord!

This distinguished structure is the meeting house for the body of believers to worship the Father eternal in the name of Jesus Christ. Ministries assigned to the members for equipping to work in service are prophets, evangelists, pastors, for the building up of the body of Christ.

Gifts and ministries differ according to the grace given each member. The steadfast in faith and love serve one another and follow Jesus' example.

Worthy to be called the house of the Lord, the shining white church stands firmly mid a lovely garden. The trees offer their budding branches and boughs to frame the color of profusion hugging each side of the pathway. The sanctuary of welcome completes the picturesque framed picture of God's call to walk as Jesus loved us ministering beyond the church.

A More Excellent Ministry - Love

MINISTRY

More Excellent Ministry   Hebrews 8:6

Creative Plan Reconciliation   2 Corinthians 5:18

Sharing Need In Service   2 Corinthians 9:12

Ministry   Heed And Fulfill Your Ministry   2 Timothy 4:5
                     Received In The Lord   Colossians 4:17

SHARING CHRIST'S SUFFERINGS   2 Corinthians 1:5

PRECIOUS PEBBLES, GEMSTONES OF WISDOM
                              1 Corinthians 2:7, Ephesians 3:9-10

EXPRESSION OF LOVE IN SERVICE TO OTHERS
     If My Disciple Love One Another   John 13:35

HOSPITALITY
     Contribute to Needs, Practicing Hospitality   John 3:16

SHARING CHRIST'S SUFFERINGS

The soul's longing to share with someone dear to the heart
Realizes frequently the absence of fulfillment.
Then as certain as sunshine returns
A ray of hope filters through the disappointing passage of time.
The gift of enlightenment is presented and there are, however briefly,
Moments to exchange places within the inner self which understand
One's own, then the other.

Jesus taught that He must suffer, and we are called for the Purpose of
Sharing His suffering as heirs of God and co-heirs with Christ.

Praying through suffering, the light of insight becomes brighter, clearer.
Through our pain Christ is near and indeed midst the nucleus.
Our heartache is the Suffering Savior.
Impossible to take your place, nor is the choice afforded as one of mine
Nevertheless, the need remains,
How can I alleviate my friend's concern.
Once again the reply from prayer
Share Christ's Suffering.

Denying the temptation to creatively design another offering of ministry
I humbly accept the scriptural direction.
Share the Suffering Christ experiences with you
Counting the honor and privilege of this intimate relationship
Among the three of us.

My prayer is that this communion remains as we continue our
Christian Journey,
Learning, growing, maturing, and reaching toward the goal

For the Prize of the High Calling of God.

As our Lord unceasingly feels every moment of doubt, each pang of fear,
Each stabbing uncertain thought of pain,
I choose to participate in sharing His Suffering with you.

PRECIOUS PEBBLES
GEMSTONES OF WISDOM

Among the Steppingstones of life, our journey,
Following the path designed, continues as
Forward we trod in faith.
Alert to clouds quietly
Appearing now to ponder.

The charted course alone seemingly terminates
For pause prompting contemplation.
Discernment
Illumines gleaming pebbles size difference increasing
Visionaries attention.

Wisdom required for new challenge.
Acknowledgment
Essential proceeding toward gain of understanding.
New and of increasing profit lies beyond the present.

Gathering gemstones within daily work, our guide is
Jesus' light through the questions, confusion, or need
He knows before we ask.

Obedience to the Word fills our very being.
Containers inadequate to compensate, cups overflowing radiate our
Hearts' joy exceedingly to occupy the abundance.

Spiritual, holy, acceptance of life's quest to seek the
Kingdom of Heaven prepares our humble gift to the
Savior adorned with the Wreath of Victory.

EXPRESSION OF LOVE
IN SERVICE TO OTHERS

Our Lord Jesus came as Suffering Savior
Made lower than the angels
Leaving His Heavenly Home
Presented as an innocent baby in a manager.

Christ chose to become Servant
Washing apostles feet and meeting others' needs
His examples to follow are
Love One Another.
Giving a cup of water
Whatever is done in service in His Name
Is presented to our Lord as gifted offering.

Loving Holy God with the heart, soul, mind,
Enables the effort to
Find time, give love, experience the power
Beyond our strength.

In obedience and humility
Thanksgiving to our Heavenly Father
Brings the reward and blessing He intended
While we bind the wounds
Warm the heart with a smile
And
Agree with God in His Purpose for our life of service
Through prayer and asking His Wisdom
Find directive each day of new life
And
The time allowed therein.

You are loved in your obedience to God.
For your caring, loving, helping, heartfelt need
To serve others,

You are loved by everyone who knows you.

May you always follow the prompting of the Holy Spirit
Through service in all you do
In the Name of Jesus.

HOSPITALITY

Generous in time, thoughtfulness
And
Found bountiful in Love,
Your gifts
Initiating from the heart
Extend to all who know you.

Blessing you glean as giving to others
Follow Jesus' example in
His Ministry.

Word

The Word of God endures everlasting to everlasting, fulfilled as it is written.

[23]*For you have been born again not of a seed which is perishable, but imperishable, that is, through the living and enduring word of God.*
1 Peter 1:23

Everlasting Word Of God
Imagery View

The living, true, pure and abiding word of God is everlasting. The implanted word received in humility is firmly set in the mind and in the spirit.

Angels perform His word obeying the voice of His word. As clearly conveyed, the scripture reveals the word remains and is preserved, a valued treasure.

Scripture is by the Holy Spirit spoken from God. Long ago He spoke in the prophets to Abraham and others. The prophecy is recorded and discovered to fulfill scripture.

The valued treasure found near the Dead Sea preserves the word of God in Scripture to remain. The story line with three symbols portrays the implanted word as purposed to become meaningful. Taking the word of God in one's inmost being, creates the story to illustrate the endurance of God's word.

A lighted space representing a framed artistic pictorial presents the display of three distinct symbols of the word of God. The urn appears as an enduring shaded metal hand crafted vase. Traces of dirt and dust mark the engraved design. The threads attached to the coal colored soils around the base of the urn denotes the place of discovery.

Lying at an angle as though raising a corner upon an elbow, the scroll of scripture finds the forefront position. The scroll rolled at the ends, seemingly to borderline the written word of God. The papyrus, or perhaps the parchment has preserved the treasured scroll.

The Holy Bible completes the display and confirms the importance of the discovery. The most valued treasure is centered between the cavern urn, the container of the scroll, and the ancient scroll preserved and remaining legible of scripture recorded prophecy for fulfillment of scripture.

Word of God
Fulfilled As Written

WORD

Word In Beginning   In The Beginning The Word   John 1:1

Living Word   The Word Of God Lives   Hebrews 4:12

Word In Scripture
         Word Lamp To My Feet A Light To My Path   Psalm 119:105

EXPERIENCES GOD'S REVEALING THE LIVING WORD
                    Established In Truth   2 Peter 1:12, 20-21

MOTHER'S THOUGHTFUL CONSIDERATION
         Absorbing Mindful Preparation For Obedient Submission
                                        Matthew 26:39, 42

PREPARATION PHASES, SUBMISSION

CONTEMPLATION- Prayerful Memories

MEDITATION- Seeking Greater Wisdom

CONSOLATION- Reflection Life Everlasting

ROBBE
     ### REACHING TOWARD PRIZE, THE HIGH
     CALLING OF GOD
     Press Toward Goal For Prize High Call   Philippians 3:14

EXPERIENCES GOD'S REVEALING
THE LIVING WORD

Golden phrase enter, intervening,
Time appearing mundane, meaningless,
Recall forthcoming gives precedence plaguing rejection.
Renewed awakened confidence
Render anticipating strides toward progressing distant sites to attain.

Abiding connection entwined insight
Hence faithfulness of Holiness seizes faltering semblance of
Thwarted misinterpretation.
Meaningless circumstances frequently questioned, found maimed.
Moments cherished extend throughout experience gleaned as
Integral reaping harmonious, peaceful, accord.
Visualizing Spiritual Purpose The Living Word, Jesus,
Becomes revealed.

Day to Day routine of moving through life's enraptured the soul
One may term experiences.
Evolving assurances strengthens faith, believing, The Word becomes alive.
Revealing our assigned lot, portion, cup, beneficial blessings.
Triumphantly thrusting forward
Victory within circumstances.

Glorious is the fresh perspective to reflect Christ.
Sobering is the realization
Warfare is at hand threading its existence throughout our life's
Weaving pattern
Introducing the Fruit of The Spirit potential encompassed by the
Protective Armour.
Oh! Such a design is the Heavenly Intent

A Personal, unlike another, plan completed
To present to Christ Our Lord.

My prayer to embrace my gift of heart's desire within the loom assigned.
To allow this intricate work uninterrupted
Faith replacing doubt, destroying disobedience, contentment
Recognizing pleasant boundaries.
Following the order of direction to meet my Creator
With a Heart of Wisdom.
The fabric of my life acceptable
Conformed to The Image of Christ.

Experiences unattended subside, diminishing growth,
Passivity prevailing.
Buds of spring nurtured emit development bursting forth in full blossoms.
Likewise one's acceptance to incidental events
Evokes the concurrence to God's fashioning a single life
His unique creation.

MOTHER'S THOUGHTFUL CONSIDERATION

Relating Personality Connotation Within
The Confines Of Expressing Visionaries.
The Absorbing Mindful Preparation For
Reaching Obedience Freedom. Submission
Please The Lord God. His Will As
Christ Prayer "Thy Will Be Done."

Based on Matthew 26:42, 26, 39

PREPARATION
SUBMISSION
PHASES

CONTEMPLATION

Prayerful Contemplation Directs
Attention Toward Memories Treasured
To Recall Compelled Recognition To
Prepare Parting Heartfelt Dearest Loved Ones.

MEDITATION

Valuable Pebble Size Gemstones Discovery
Increases Depth Of Spiritual Insight Prompting
Meditation Seeking Greater Wisdom.

CONSOLATION

Quiet Waters Console The Inner Being
Of The Soul
As The Lily Pads Move To And Fro
Reflecting Jesus' Beauty Overshadowing
The Valleys We Know Below.

CONTEMPLATION

Twilight approaches within the shadows of memories remaining.
Lovely visions appear clearly to recall
New Life in Christ redeemed through His atoning blood
Spiritual unity with loving wife to join family
God gifted beautiful daughter child's call voicing "Daddy"
Adorable baby son to follow preceding footsteps
Led by the Savior.

Equity in time alloted family known before
During childhood playtime, sibling fun,
Love, security, and parents' care,
Joining extended family for revealed secrets
Laughter of joy and delightful children's
Response of enthusiastic interest.

Abounding grace illumines season of response
Hope confirmed increasingly present
Reality perceived through gracious mercy
For hearing the summons from heavenly places.

Come for your place awaits.
Faith produces endurance for completion
Prepared your submissive reply
Parting from earthly dwelling brings perfection
Promised through time denied rejection.

Prayer for obedience to the Word
Submission desire to become same as that which is God's will.

Here I Am Lord.

MEDITATION

Known before Holy God consecrated my life
I reaching partial cup.

Days planned lifted to shelter on high.
The path of life revealed
Pleasant places provided
Personal measure of faith allotted.
Steppingstones for designed journey
Illuminated from Jesus' Lighthouse
Course for intended abundant blessings
Sounds the call for necessary redirection.

Encounters, divine appointments, adversities
Appear and present questionable confusion
Yet our guide through spiritual wisdom
Intervenes for reckoning
Seemingly overwhelming obstacles.
Halting the complacent acquire routine,
Self reliant, satisfied comfort zone.

Lord! Only darkness surrounds my portion
Without consciousness
My being is strangely silent.
Isolation pervades.
The Savior's footprints fade
Along this unfamiliar trodden way.

CONSOLATION

Within quiet time continuing thoughts
Move toward quests for sensing
Heavenly father remains near
Hear my cry
Draw me closer Lord.

Fatigue, pain, awareness, concerns I know
Encouragement then Improvement
Presently absence returns.
This invasion aggressively forwards
Along the march of passing hours
Enduring season soon to change.

My faith looks up to Thee
Your light to follow beckons me
Calvary's cross I see.
Renewed strength generously awakens
Trust placed within the Spirit sealed
Christ hanging on His chosen tree.
Pouring out His atoning blood
I see. I see.
Just for me now in this my agony.

Your face I seek to persevere to claim my faith.
Endurance severe as essential
The plan to receive completion
For perfection granted to be conformed
To the image of Christ
His only begotten Son
The Image of The Invisible God.

153

ROBBE

REACHING TOWARD THE PRIZE
THE HIGH CALLING OF GOD

Family gathers to celebrate reaffirm and pray
Increasing number attendance abounding love
Awareness depth of discovery appreciate
Spiritual insight God ordained Legacy.

Our Bryans House Reflects
Absence of loved ones among remaining to serve
Declining health intervenes our thoughts
Our heartfelt concern to share pain.
Wisdom granted to share Christ's sufferings
As He shares suffering with ones in need.

Time Is Precious
Presently to care intensely through all
Prompting direction for obedience pleasing
The Most High plan and fulfilling
Our Creator's ultimate design of love.

Preparation ordered for submission
Beautiful sounding call heard
Midst fragrance and sweet aroma
Blessed voice of dearest Name above all.

Robbe Come Home

Confirmation

Truth is established. The gospel is carried and preached throughout the world to all creation. While the Lord worked with them, the Word was confirmed by the signs that followed.

Based on Mark 16:20

Confirmation of the Gospel
Imagery View

To balance Life's scale of Confirmation of the gospel, the weight of Truth and Testimonies is equal. The word of the living God is truth, enduring and everlasting.

Following the resurrection of Jesus Christ our Lord, He met with the eleven apostles and gave to them the great commission. Preach the gospel to all creation, making disciples of all nations, Jesus challenged. Importantly He added, baptizing them in the name of the Father, the Son, and the Holy Spirit.

The disciples who had walked with the Lord the three years of His earthly ministry, were scattered, as Jesus had told them.

The eleven friends of Jesus, though separated from each other, preached everywhere. The work of the first gospel preachers was blessed by God and He confirmed the word by signs that followed.

There were some preaching from envy and strife, and proclaiming Christ within their own ambition. Nevertheless, the appointed ones for the defense of the gospel were preaching Christ from good will and out of love. These defenders of the gospel revealed God's confirming the truth in the word with an oath.

The gospel truth is confirmed in the word. An oath confirms and ends every dispute. The unchangeableness of God's purpose is confirmed with an oath.

Book Signing
Reception

You are cordially invited
To attend Annette Bryan's
Celebration of sharing her new book
"Walk With Me - God's Call to the Church".

Join with family and friends
Saturday June Third
From One o'clock to Three o'clock.

Eastside Baptist Church
Student Center
Lower Roswell Rd.
Marietta, Georgia

Enjoy The Panorama Replica Display
Path of Life's Journey.

Books available for personal
Commemorative Inscription.

RSVP
Annette
770-971-2047
or Robin McGaha
email sissy40@gmail.com

Gospel Confirmed

CONFIRMATION

Confidence Work Begun in You He Will Perfect It · Philippians 1:6

Christ Confirmed Promises Given to Fathers · Romans 15:8

Gospel Truth Confirmed in the Word · Mark 16:20

Confirmation: Grace Given Those Jesus Confirms
To the End Blameless · 1 Corinthians 1:8

TEARS   Heart of Compassion · Colossians 3:12

TEARS REJOICE · Romans 12:15

TEARS FOR THE CHILD · Psalm 56:8

TEARS FOR MY PAIN OF LOSS PRAISE FOR MY GAIN - CHILDREN · Jeremiah 29:11

TEARS OF SORROW · James 4:6

FRIENDSHIP REGENERATION · Romans 12:3, 2 Corinthians 12:9

TEARS

There are distinct tears for the pain experienced, endured and suffered
As one alone must bear.
Significantly one sheds tears for another in appreciation of the
Other person's concern
Perhaps not recognized before sharing.
The hopelessness seen for lonely elderly when neglected or abandoned.
Children expressing their need for attention and love.
The meekness and humbleness reflective of Jesus' example.
Sacrament of Communion
In obedience to our Lord's command to
Remember His body and blood freely He gave to forgive our sins.

For the Lost
The unsaved, those separated from our Holy God.
Tears of heart wrenching magnitude surface in compulsive contrition
For God's dear created who know not the security held personally for each
Only to claim our position as co-heirs with Christ.

For Grandparents
Never to have known the Grandmother or Grandfather
Who through their profession of faith in our Lord left an inheritance
For their children's children recorded in Proverbs 13:22.
Tears inhabit my soul for the parents and grandparents
Who were unable to know.
The blessed person God so graciously, never ceases to love,
And works in me
Both to desire and to do His Will
Only through the magnificent power of the Holy Spirit.
There are tears for Grandchildren and their Grandparents and
Great Grandparents

Who knew not each other.
I weep for my children's children and great grandchildren I may not see
Until we join at the Throne of God and worship together
Jesus our Lord.

Forget Not My Tears
Another promise from God the Father.
All are listed in His Scroll and recorded.
He knows my weeping and recalls my tears.

We are reminded that He has seen each droplet and beckons
Cast your cares upon Me.
For he who sows in tears will reap in rejoicing.
Our Father comforts us, so we in turn may
Share Christ's sufferings.
Comfort each other and bear one another's burdens.

Pent Emotions
Escape with tears of joy while sharing with another
A celebrated reply to requested need.
Then accepting the denotation of answer to find
Release from harnessed feelings
Seemingly held in abeyance for the appropriate moment to
Connect the experience.
Bearing one another's burden lends the definition in willingness
To allow another to carry a load portion
Relieving the weight and assuming hope for encouragement.

TEARS REJOICE

Rejoice
Intermingling our tears
Let us express our gratitude in obedience
Give thanks in all things:
Within the pain of heartbreak.
Hopefulness in visualizing harmony.
Darkened distress.
The glimpsing light of truth.
Times of joyfulness.
Seasons of sorrow.
Exhilarated gladness.
Moments of doubt.
Assurance we are sealed with the Holy Spirit
Validating security.

Human Kindness
Bring surfacing tears acknowledging man's sense and compelling
Urgency toward giving.
The human spirit reaching toward God revealed opportunity
Overflows into acceptance of forgiveness
Discovered through confession and remorse.
Tears appear within the freedom of quiet, satisfied, repentance
Within conclusion of praise offering.
Sacrificial thanksgiving joins the Gift Provider
At the alter of worship.
As the only One worthy to pronounce absolution meets the petitioner
Assurance of righteousness through the removal of sin
Is established as far as the East is from the West.
Renewal sustained.

Awesomeness
Produce the tears expressing visually the inability to
Verbalize or explain fully
The extent of the overwhelming
Inner being exultation.

Self-Expressive
Tears reveal the God given desire to experience more intimately
The Holy Trinity.
The One and Only Jehovah God
Who has balanced life with the free will and choice of man
And
The omnipotent God controlled universe in its entirety.
God the son, Messiah, Savior for all.
God the Holy Spirit given to indwell the repentant believer.

Acknowledgment
In God's continuous work in and through our lives among the nations
Lends place for tears within effectual timing.
Recognizing answered prayer provides the tears of acknowledgment
Proclaiming our heavenly Father who fulfills His plan for enduring time
The Purpose of His Heart through all generations
Recorded in Psalm 33:10

Insight
Culminates in tears
As illuminating light increases visual comprehension.
Direction is clarified and more clearly understood.

TEARS FOR THE CHILD

The Child
God's crowning glory to His creation's beauty when He said,
"Let Us make man in Our own image."
An innocence, a purity of marvelous
Perfection in the mind of Christ
In the heart of God.

A Baby to Hold
To feel the wonder of the presently small person he or she will
Always remain
Until the transformation following completion of life's
Designed, Planned, Assignment.
This child who becomes spiritually born again.

The Little One
Owns his heart for suffering, disappointment, pain, hurt,
Perhaps anger, or need from abuse.
Streaming tears flow endlessly when a child's anguish
Cannot be altered.

Tears
For the children wrench the heart.
The face reflects the agony unveiled when awareness shines the light
Upon the tortured child.
The soul weeps for a little one whose need is unmet.

The Holy Spirit
Within me grieves with my mourning a child's loss
However seemingly small.
However monumental.

Through Flooding Tears
I sense the comfort of knowing God is in control.
He allows not one droplet from a precious child's eyes escape
His gathering the pools of heartache
Into His very own assigned place within the secure healing
Found only in Jesus our Lord.

We Weep for the Children
As God holds them very closely to Himself.
Each is counted and known by his or her name.
A child, innocent, pure, blameless, and dearly valuable
As life itself and precious in the sight of God
Permeates the heart of the Holy Creator.

Accumulation of the Child's
Sadness, weeping, as he feels excluded or friendless or unaccepted
Registers with God the Father more intensely
When the Child frequently is viewed by insensitivity
Only as a shadow.

The Celestial Parent
Advances His plan to reverse the child's feelings of rejection.
Working in him to impart security only available and residing
In the Most High.

TEARS FOR MY PAIN OF LOSS
PRAISE FOR MY GAIN

CHILDREN

Communication disappearing, identified with my children
Has produced many tears.
All bottled and reserved in God's care.

Were there three wishes granted, I could entertain no regrets.
Only pleasant, fun and blessed memories
Would pervade my thoughts and recollections while visions of
Robbe, Craig, and Elyse, fill my heart
Upon each prompting to remember
My loving, wonderful, precious, children.

Midst recalling moments of misunderstanding
God has redirected my steps along His ordained passage
For my Christian maturing.

Through loss of communicating, fellowship,
The altered course has revealed direction toward acquiring
The desired goal for my ultimate achievement.

Resting within my trusting God
Believing His Word
Reassurance granted in my hope is in
His Covenant Promise.
Within the divine care and protection
As all things work together for good for those who love God
We who are called according to His purpose.

I pray that upon each recurring tearful experience for
Pain of Loss with my children
The Holy Spirit will bring to mind the gain of communication with
Holy God
Resounding in Praise To His Name.

TEARS OF SORROW

The sudden appearance of moisture upon my cheeks
Accompanies the question
What is this which has come to request my consideration.

Thoughts begin racing through my memory recalling those
Suppressed moments
Preferred to submerge beyond recognition.
Now the dampness demands the allowance of identification.
The insistent pangs of remorseful scenes.

My regret cannot be retrieved.
Self-forgiveness alone can appease
The sincere sorrow for the expressed ungratefulness
Upon receiving a beautiful, sincerely thoughtful gift
Unlike my anticipated expectation.
Sighing relief permits a short reprieve from my heart's pain.

Then another visionary captures the increasing tearful flow.
I recall an occasion enjoying an excursion with my loving brother.
Opportunity passed to consider his needs or feelings.
The heartache of selfishness is too much to bear.
The neglect cannot be rectified.
Years of attempt to erase the wounded spirit have not been successful.

The source and supply for weeping seemingly becomes uninterrupted.
Pain my children suffered from apathetic, uninterested, insensitive
Decisions
Effected by others
Present once more my helplessness to replace their devastation.

Intensely I become aware of dependence upon our Heavenly Father
To work all things together for good
Placing all confidence in His Word of Truth
He will meet all our needs.

I visualize my son's teacher separating him from his class and he felt all
Alone.
Again there is the assurance of God is in control
The child senses my compassion
Later the peace of healing from the Heavenly Father.

Nevertheless I believe my heart will surely break into many pieces
Each time incidents are summoned to mind
Whenever my child's need has been unmet
Unaware until impossible to comfort
As he or she shed tears I cannot share or cause to disappear with
Understanding.

God is good to repeatedly give insight for the knowledge and consistent
Assurance of healing available in our Lord Jesus
As He accomplishes all these matters that concern us.
The experience in which my child was neglected by my
Misinterpretation of his concern.
Praise the Lord for this child's forgiving heart.

Prayer without ceasing brings conviction
My greatest concern and deepest sorrow
With immensity of weeping profusely
Finds the assigned place within the realm of intercessory request.
That one who is lost, separated from the
Holy Trinity
Comes to the cross

Believing Jesus is the Son of God
Repenting of sin
Asking forgiveness
Accepting Jesus Christ as personal Lord and Savior.

FRIENDSHIP REGENERATION

Friendships seemingly dissolved present heartache
An indescribable loss permeating
The soul unfulfilled.
Ah! Overwhelmingly peaceful contentment
Slowly to cover the absence once cherished then
Fading in the distance.
Time passes. Healing occurs. Soul and heart agree.
The Joseph's Principle enlightens my comprehension.
Yet another promise from the Word.

For whatever reason my friendship rejected
God meant it for good
And works all things together for His purpose.
Praise His Holy Name!

For every loss as the disappearance from the heart
A shattered dream, a sunset darkened
A new day is presented in the morning.
There! The changing colors throughout the sky
From fading shadows
To lights of promise for a new beginning of life
To be held with the hope of joy
The sunrise in all its glory.

This is my praise to The Creator of sunset loss
Gain of sunrise gift, our very existence.
Who has filled my heart and life
With friendship.

Reconciliation

[20a]God through Christ reconciled the world to Himself. [22]Christ has now reconciled you in His fleshly body through death in order to present you before God holy and blameless and beyond reproach.

Colossians 1:20a, 22

Reconciliation, Bonded Unity Restored
Imagery View

Man, yet unaware his life's path, will continue leading toward the cross of Jesus. There the Ultimate distance between God and man is bridged through God's purpose of forthcoming Reconciliation. Complete unity is restored which was established from the beginning.

It was the Father's pleasure, through Christ, to reconcile all things to Himself.

Having made peace through His cross, and through His fleshly body in death, Christ reconciled God and man. Restoring Holy God's established unity with man, preparation has accomplished. For Christ to present before the Father those who are holy blameless, and beyond reproach.

The word of the cross, eternal life, provides salvation to the repentant redeemed through the power of the cross proclaimed.

God's Bonded
Unity Restored

RECONCILIATION

God Reconciled All Things Through Christ　　　　Colossians 1:19-20

God Gave Us The Ministry Of Reconciliation

　　　　　　　　　　　　　　　　　　　　2 Corinthians 5:18

And Committed To Us The Word Of Reconciliation

　　　　　　　　　　　　　　　　　　　　2 Corinthians 5:19

Reconciliation　　　　　　　　　　　　　2 Corinthians 5:19
　　　God In Christ Reconciled The World To Himself

AT THE CROSS　　　　It Is Finished　　　　　　John 19:30

LOVELY COMPASSION OF HOLINESS
　　　Rejoice In God Through Christ We Receive Reconciliation
　　　　　　　　　　　　　　　　　　　　　Romans 5:11
　　　　　　BROTHER'S FAMILY GATHERING
　　　　　　　　Love One Another　　　　　John 15:12

　　　　SIBLINGS ENDEARMENT
　　　　　　　　Friend Brother　　　　　Proverbs 18:24

　　　　LOST FOUND REDEEMED
　　　Seasons Pass Hope Wanted Son Was Dead Now He Lives
　　　　　　　　　　　　　　　　　　　　　Luke 15:24

AT THE CROSS

Visual reflection moves love within
Surfacing as sensory nudgings
Attempt to repress the tense moment.
Perceived hearing shares suffering my Savior's
Pain alone the peace for my gain.

His nail print hands the view appears
Clutching heart-felt anguish unlike
That Christ could bear.
Slumbering aimlessly
How long time season unknown.

New lighting I see shadowing Jesus
Hanging before me.

God's work circulating His being
Portraying shame for world to gage.
Purposed unity restored
Man's need secured throughout eternity.

Repentance commitment made
Mercy granted generously sin debt paid
Through atoning blood the immaculate
Sacrificial offering accomplished.
Pardon received freedom in forgiveness
Reconciliation fulfilled.

It Is Finished.
His final words remain for hearing
Spoken to pervade the heart

Upon walking truth forward carry.
Following Jesus envisioning
Our Lord's cross at calvary
CRUCIFIED.

A LOVELY COMPASSION OF HOLINESS

BROTHERS FAMILY GATHERING

Marriages, homes, and children, became new responsibilities, blessings,
Disappointments, and, failure seemed to follow.
Still God's Hand, Our Heavenly Father's Heart
The unchangeable constant sustain life, recovery, reconciliation.
Oh! The inadequacy to pen the gratitude Holy God knew each of us before
Formation, Life, Birth!
Yet more awesome, the provision through Christ's atoning blood,
Salvation.
How humbly to learn one's identity
Through the imparting of God's wisdom.

As an individual, expressing Mother, expressing Daddy,
As each of us have become
Part of the whole of two divinely chosen parents.

Comprising this new generation,
We first cousins find indescribable joy recalling having known our
Dad's brothers.
Bonding, and connecting, brings pleasure unaccountable through words.
Time is the essence of recovering lost years.
Now the opportunity to revel in the uncertain moments remaining
We may share
Appear urgently calling to reserve recent memories' dearest treasures.

Since 1929 upon our grandmother Ruby's death
The families of the Wilson Brothers, our Dads, have been scattered
Over our country. Separated as relatives,
Unknown to each other, and to our Dad's sisters Betty and Sarah.

Only through the keen interest and loving care of our Uncle Bo, and
Now our dear Aunt Lottie,
Has communication been accomplished among our families
And especially the endearing relationship among
Granddaddy Wilson's daughters Betty and Sarah.
Committed to the preservation of the dignity of memory for each
Of our parents and grandparents
The tribute is lovingly made to each one.

It is written that Granddaddy loved all his children and with
Integrity and defense of character
He established and proclaimed truth and honor for the Wilson name.
God's gift of beauty and standard for the banner we carry forth in life
Our name.

Granddaddy compassionately responded to Uncle Ed's humble request
For assistance during illness.
How deeply seeded is the confidence we relate our need to the
Hope in parents.
Often, however, fulfillment is repeatedly, denied or rejected.

Sibling relation spanned the years with great distance between encounters.
Following Uncle Ed's prolonged absence, Sarah asked to place an ad in
The newspaper for her brother.

Uncle Bo visited his sisters and their Mother, Mamma Wilson, after
Granddaddy's death
As frequently as possible, as he was concerned for his sisters and
Brothers' families.
Once the two brothers and families traveled to Selma together.
My first recollection of Sarah is synonymous with her welcoming gift
Of a blue velvet hair band.

She was impressed the little twins enjoyed the early morning sounds of
Singing birds.

Betty visited with us in Brookhaven, allowing brother Howard to
Reciprocate the hospitality,
Entertaining, and, souvenir photographs.

A LOVELY COMPASSION OF HOLINESS

SIBLING ENDEARMENTS

Uncle Ed's Louise and Buddy blessed with wonderful families
As Clarence's and George's families enthrall their anticipating of
Continued growth and spiritual
Aspiration presently and until the Lord comes for us.
Not the least of which they all enjoy their welcome into the family
As though never absent.

Uncle Bo's Roberta, Bill, and Jim had such a short time with their
Sweet, loving, Dad.
However, Daddy's youngest brother's influence greatly impacted my
Life as many others
Expressed through his integrity, and sensitive, forgiving spirit.
Memories recall his teaching to me thoughtfulness, and kindness,
Along with being appreciative.
Few knew the depth his love of God and Country, as he repeatedly
Requested to serve within his capabilities.

Howard, Daddy, loved each of his four children,
Always emphasizing equity.
Suffering the loss of one in death, he felt the pain more intensely
Within that reserved heart's place
Remaining vacant with failure to know his first born.
We know today he would rejoice with us
Bob is happy we have found him.
Pain of loss increased the profound strength of deepening,
Penetrating, love for his children.
We know not how, yet we found one day followed another.
God's generosity once again showered us as Bob and his family

Complete Don's and my family.
Donald and Ronald had been inseparable.
I as one among the children three still apart from that enjoyment
Personalities known as the twins.
Stunned beyond comprehension, I became useless to comfort or minister.
Only God's Grace was set in place to cover us
To meet Donald's need, understanding, his overwhelming grief,
Sufficient to sustain this child.

Ten first cousins, collectively, separately, sharing pain, loss, disappointment.
Learning through years of holy wisdom
The healing of forgiveness, the joy of love, gratitude of obedience.
Now in autumn of life the renewal of strength soaring as eagles
Once again a good and perfect gift that only reaches the heart of humility
From Heaven above.

We offer our sacrifice of praise
To our Lord and Savior
For truly our family reunion is A Lovely Compassion of Holiness.

A LOVELY COMPASSION OF HOLINESS

LOST FOUND REDEEMED

A lifetime in season passed seemingly.
Our family of three now excitedly met the Air Force Ship from Alaska.
The band played. We waved. Our hearts skipped beats.
Sarah, John, Scott, and Glenn stepped toward us.

Experiencing family relations was new and thrilling.
Someone insisted there was no question.
Seven persons in a three room apartment.
The only southern arrangement to consider with space to spare for
Uncle Howard to polish his nephews' shoes.

The quest for Louise's and Buddy's Dad, and perseverance became
Blessed and fruitful.
God answered as she and Marvin searched for many years to follow
Scripture Honor your parents
Rewarded, however, with God's purpose in His timing of fifty years.
Only through the intervening of Our Lord, Clarence, George, and
Bob, have been brought to join us.

Oh! To read the letter that Uncle Ed wrote professing Christ, finding
Salvation, and
Asking forgiveness from his family as necessary for Eternal Peace
And Presence with Holy God.
Who can absorb the magnitude of God's love and grace
Translating His forgiveness and requiring the same from us for each other.

Allow the little children to come to me, remains Jesus' bidding
Essentially each one must accept Christ with the faith of a child.

That of believing God's Word.

As the alter call was given each Sunday, two little boys responded
To Jesus' calling, "Come Follow Me."
The loving, understanding, pastor patiently welcomed Howard and his
Little brother Bo each week.
Just as we know our Lord accepts and welcomes each one every time
We call on His Name.

Oh! Were we permitted to grant the heart's desire.
To soothe the pangs of despairing hope. See our disappointments
Disappear from the unrequited expectations of parents.
Dreams attained, realized within our searching.
This too was not to be owned.
Choosing life's path of success midst one's perspective leads beyond
The charted course ordained to accomplish steps toward
The High Calling of God.

Christ was intended to suffer, we as His co-heirs to share
His sufferings, as He suffer with each of us.
A gift of selected ministry pales in comparison to the incomparable joy
Sharing Christ's Suffering.

Worship

[28]*Therefore, since we receive a kingdom which cannot be shaken, let us show gratitude, by which we may offer to God an acceptable service with reverence and awe.*

Hebrews 12:28

Worship Acceptable & Pleasing to God
Imagery View

A child praying portrays he and God are having a conversation.

The pictured little boy clasps together his small hands and bows his head naturally. The early tendency toward reverence appears reflective in faith that children's prayers are offered believing God hears.

Moreover, small hands increasing in size fold together within the attitude of thanksgiving and seeking assurance. In time, hands develop for work, service, offering and worshipful prayer. Associated with one's own world, hope and security mingle among varied desires and requests presented in prayer. Faith and trust increase and leads to worship.

The faith of a child is to pray as he believes God hears his prayer. The humbleness of Jesus' little ones leads to trust in their prayerful worship.

The simple prayer from the heart is offered in trust. Believing God's hearing and reply, the little boy's faith is confirmed.

True Worshiper's Offerings
Pleasing To God

WORSHIP

Fear Of The Lord Is Clear Endures Forever   Psalm 19:9

Offer To God Acceptable Service With Reverence And Awe

Hebrews 12:28

Through His Sacrifice Of Praise In Thanks To God To His Name

Hebrews 13:15

WORSHIP

> Then Jesus said, "for it is written you shall Worship the Lord your God, and serve Him only."

Matthew 13:15

CHRIST'S COURAGE PLEASING GOD
> Not As I Will But As Thy Wilt   Matthew 26:39

GRATITUDE IN OBEDIENCE
Presenting Living Sacrifice Worship   Romans 5:11

MUSIC
> For You Will Go Out With Joy Lead Forth With Peace. Mountains And Hills Shout With Joy And Trees Clap Their Hands.

Isaiah 55:12

WORSHIP

In Honor, Praise, Thanksgiving,
And Tribute
With Reference, Fear
And Awesome Wonder
The Lord God Almighty
Receives The Approach
Of One's Offering.
Expression Of Feeble Attempt
Worthy Tribute Presented.
Accepted As His Own Planned,
Purposed, Good Pleasure.

CHRIST'S COURAGE
PLEASING GOD

Our Lord Jesus becoming man
Willingly assumed the human body
Picturesque of the foreshadowing of sharing pain, fear, long suffering
His chosen bride's every concern.

Exemplifying the perfect multiple character qualities essential for
Conformity to Christ's image
We learn the desired response to each of life's circumstances.

From childhood aware of His
Need to be about the Heavenly Father's business
Courage for proclaiming truth became eminent.

Led by the Holy Spirit for Baptism as example
Jesus then presented courage providing strength through the
Awesome wilderness temptation to rescind His commitment.
The resounding response illustrated
I Rebuke You Satan!

Following, the teaching, healing, ministering years Christ
Our God incarnate
Our suffering Savior
The Son of man
Summoned courage, preserving in
Appearance of hopelessness and disappointment.

Boldly through the power of the Holy Spirit
The epitome of Jesus' courage is infinitely visionary.
The trial, blasphemous accusations,

The agonizing prayer garden, the cross.
Victory! Praise The Lord! Courage!

A gifted spiritual enabling conqueror our defeat.
Birth of New Hope
New life in Christ.

My gratitude extends to you and your family
For sharing your deepest concern
Allowing the personification of
Courage.

GRATITUDE
IN OBEDIENCE

Oh to express my innermost need
To sacrificially express my gratitude
Success through every avenue of attempt.

Failure returns to prayer searching.
Gradual enlightenment translates to calming, peaceful, serenity.
Provision available presently
There turning to view the distant past as well.

Is desire always first to fill the questioning space of thought.
Will source of truth ever
Spring to mind quickly as the heart of purity
The cleanliness of sin forgiveness
Allows spiritual insight to supply and satisfy the soul's yearning.

Yes. Sight is clear. Hearing sound. Understanding bestowed.
God's wisdom imparted throughout His holy word.
Obedience He requires rather than sacrifice.
How, Lord, in my weak incapable accomplishment,
Am I to rely upon advice of those known as wise.

Praise The Lord!
The Holy Spirit will teach meaning.
His intercessory prayers enable the seeking heart to glorify Christ

Praise The Lord!

MUSIC

Created composition intangible, yet an integral interspersing
Well enmeshed among the senses.
Melodious strains become visionary through one's
Sight of beauty
Perceived within fields of floral profusion.

Hear heart the arrangement of the
Score of rolling seas of scales
The solace of wind chiming notes
The thundering chords marvelously united in harmony.

Oh! The fragrant interlude of the soul's enraptured exhilaration
A rhapsody recalled.
Taste the symphony's delectable means permitting the sense of rhythm
Circulating other stimulated awareness of gratification.
Touch incomparable phrasing becoming personal experience
To find its treasure chest for pleasurable reminiscence.

God given sixth sense of sharing.
Can this explain our Lord's intention for
Music orchestration,
Our privilege likewise to
Another give?

Security

[22] Christ has now reconciled you in His fleshly body through death in order to present you before God holy and blameless and beyond reproach.

Colossians 1:22

Resurrection Security
Imagery View

Eternal Life

Break of dawn announced eternal life with the Lord Jesus Christ. The garden where Jesus had been brought for burial, had become picturesque as the shadows parted. The fading darkness of night's despair encompassing the crucifixion, allowed the sunlight of hope for the two women approaching the tomb for their Lord's body.

The tomb was open, and the large heavy stone had been rolled away for the angel prominent sitting position. The two friends had ministered to the Lord Jesus as He had hung on His cross. The suffering Savior's atoning blood had flowed from His body over His feet and to the ground for the standing ones to see.

At first sight of the open tomb, the women in astonishment feared Jesus' body had been stolen. The angel from heaven splendidly dressed in his snow white garment proclaimed with great joy: He is not here. He is risen. Jesus lives.

We also will live. Whoever believes in Me. I am the resurrection and eternal life.

Eternal Life's Assurance

SECURITY

Righteous Man Safe In Name Of The Lord   Psalm 18:10-11

Walk In My Statutes And Commandments, Live Securely
                                              Leviticus 26:5

Whatever Under The Whole Of Heavens Is Mine   Job 4:11

SECURITY
The Father Qualified Us Share in Inheritance of Saints in Life
    The World After Grace, Give You the Inheritance Among Sanctified
                          Colossians 1:12, Romans 8:29, James 1:5

JOURNEY TOGETHER
                    Give To You   Matthew 26:29

WEALTH OF GRACE IMPARTED
    Obey My Voice, Keep My Covenant, Be My Own Possession
                                              Exodus 19:5

SECURITY

Sovereign Author of Security. The Ordained
Superlative Gift is Held in Treasury to be Presented
Before Him Holy and Blameless and Beyond
Reproach. Each Chosen One Awaits This
Highest Honor Yet Completing God's Proposed
Plan.

Within Life's Journey Called to Follow
The Phases of Preparation Afford Obedience to
Be Conformed to the Image of His Son. Confidence
Increases as Wisdom Through Scripture Abounds.
Faith Endowed Perseverance Applied, Hope
Received, Security Acquired.

JOURNEY TOGETHER

Afore unknown Christ's submission
The immaculate sacrificial lamb
Offer acceptable
Required payment sin debt
Sufficiently satisfied.

Mid sensing own debt pardoned
Contrite heart bowing in praise offering
Dispels overshadowing guilt
To present insignificant one freely
Privileged gift tribute to make.

In honor for
The only God our Savior.
Glory, majesty, worthy,
Declare His wondrous works
All earth and heaven.
Bless His holy name
Now, forever, and throughout eternity.

Grace directs the path to love, scripture,
Knowledge of the Heavenly order,
Wisdom of truth, and justice.

Voice of familiar thought it seems
Heard and attention held
Within quiet slumbering time alone
Softly beckoning
Yet clearly comprehensive
Come walk with Me.

WEALTH OF GRACE IMPARTED

Established within infinite existence
Possessions of ownership display
Throughout the sphere of view
While circulating the magnificent expanse

Gifts of grandeur allotted chosen one favored
Provision creation's portion glimpse to receive.
Filled with awesome amendment
Splendid beauty incites
Pleasantries extended then returned.

Proposed work of mystery to be revealed.
Time released plan for fellow-heir
Ordained will of the Heavenly Father.
Man's legacy God's desire
Through Christ's self sacrifice
To accomplish the works ordained plan
The intended purpose fulfilled.

Only Begotten Son given for all who believe
For the lost, the found, those sought,
The justified proven deserved.
Flight escapes peril of death
Shared possession eternal life remain unending.

Redeemed to glorify Jesus
Amazed the brilliance to perceive
Works the Most High many reaching
His praise greatly forwards
Far beyond horizons mightily portrayed.

Saints precious in His name an inheritance
Of the Lord
Now claim exalted seating in the heavenly places.

⁶the one who says that he remains in Him ought, himself also, walk just as He walked.

1 John 2:6

⁴Therefore we have been buried with Him through baptism into death, so that, just as Christ was raised from the dead through the glory of the Father, so we too may walk in newness of life.

Romans 6:4

WALK WITH ME

Envision wonders performed greater
Grandeur yet revealed
Far beyond the universal expanse
Comprehension to behold permitted
My favored one lovingly perceive.

Following the charted course
Prepare faith refined
Healing hope sustained
Love enduring refrain in beauty supremely
Praise sounding alone our
Savior Jesus Name.

Along life's journey the quest to see
Ford streams to quiet paths
Then move through rafting rivers
Gathering strength bridges leading
Destinations unseen.

There the peaks above await
The pressing climb to reach
Horizons reveal the sovereign possessions
For His good pleasure
To bequeath.

The End

There is no ending..........

There is no ending.......

Life's Path steppingstone Security affords the assurance for which the quest was sought. Stretching farther than the visible range allows, the charted path leads to all that God has prepared for those who love Him. Continuous as the eternal God, whose paths are made straight. Once again the resounding call is heard.

The daily commitment time shared with the Lord confirms clearly the Path of Life is continuous to follow, heeding God's call. Walk With Me forever.

Amidst these wondrous steps of grace along the pathway unfolds the unfathomed depth of God's everlasting Love which He has prepared to reveal. The poetic beauty of Love remains within Life's quest toward the goal for the prize. The search is constant, as the aspiring walk renews the heart, refines faith, and hope abides.

The Love of God everlasting, continues unfolding to illuminate Life's path with the Light of the world. The experiences of wisdom gained along the Journey, reveal greater insight to Walk With Me forever.

Onward

Things which eye has not seen and ear has not heard and which have not entered the heart of man all that God has prepared for those who love Him.

1 Corinthians 2:9

The Lord is near, abiding evermore. His paths are made straight for walking the utmost distance.

Milestone experiences are available, the threads within the fabric of Life are connected. Thus, the works equipped, and the fabric pattern nearing completion, calls for other phases of the Preparation.

Commitment reply to daily walk along the journey path, incites a resurgent need of wisdom. The pebble size stones of wisdom are discovered among the Genre steppingstones of the Path of Life. Whereas the implanted word of God is found to be imparted in His purposed timing.

Once again the Charted guideline offers direction for the search to commence Anticipation to touch all that is planned, fills the inmost desire to continue the Journey. The commitment made early on confirms the seeking steps advancing toward all that God has prepared.

Press onward to be found holy, blameless, beyond reproach, to be presented before the Heavenly Father.

Additional Reflections for your
Inspiration

INSPIRATION

For What Does the Scripture Say, Believed God and It Was
Reckoned To Him as Righteousness.

Romans 4:3

A Wreath Of Salvation Wisdom and Knowledge the Fear of the Lord is
His Treasure.   Isaiah 33:6

For Where Your Treasure Will Your Heart Be Also.

Matthew 6:21

In Whom Christ Himself are Hidden All Treasure Of Wisdom and
Knowledge.

Colossians 2:3

To Be Complete Follow Me And You Shall Have Treasure In Heaven
Matthew 19:21

INSPIRATION   Colossians 1:12
And Do Not Neglect Doing Good And Sharing
For Such Sacrifices God Is Pleased.
The Inheritance Among Sanctified
Led To Set Words To Paper Through Brief Attention
To Thought, Varied Ideas Seemingly
Assumed Form. The Meaning Concluding
Lines And Verse, Appeared To Convey A Connection.
Sensing The Intention Had Not Been Met
For The Occasion Ending Determined.

HOPE   Comfort

WHITEBLOSSOM   Hope

REDBUDS   Pursue Truth

216

RETURNED LOVE   Worship

TWILIGHT REFLECTIONS   Meditation

COMMITTED CARING   Praise Offering

RAINBOW OF PROMISES   Vow Fulfillment

MUSIC   Singing Tribute

LIGHTHOUSE   Encouragement

GOD GIVEN SENSITIVITY   Faith

SHARING   Affirmation

FRIENDS   Valued Treasure

INSPIRATION

The Fear Of The Lord Is His Treasure

Treasured Possession To Cherish
And Search Its Assessment
Shielding The Prized Gift Safely
Guard Its Worth
Enhances The Value For Offering
Greater Tribute To Honor The Contributor
Worthy To Be Praised.

For Whatever Was Written in Earlier Times
Was Written For Our Instruction,
So That Through Perseverance And The
Encouragement Of The Scriptures
We Might Have Hope.

Romans 15:4

HOME

My dwelling place presently provided
The space my heart can rejoice
Immersed in warmth of security.

Open to share with all
Inhabited within the love, laughter,
Concerns pondered by the hearth
And
Those times of sadness requiring
An outstretched hand.

Through near or apart
Prayer and well wishes extend
From my humble abode to yours
In your time of need.

ANNETTE BRYANS

WHITE BLOSSOM

As the heavy blanket of snow falls silently
To cover the hardened, crusted,
Earthen surface
Cold and bone chilling despair
May overwhelm the soul.

Then the pleading heart searches
Seasons' change to glimpse
Blossoms of white push above ground
So forbidding afore,
Now lending strength for hope,
Gratefulness for grace.
God's freely generous gift.

RED BUDS

Defying legend of the tree
Visions of the floral disclosure exposing to view
Capture the heart's delight
Taking pleasure in the Creator's Purpose to
Behold His Beauty.

Though friendship once betrayed
The Red Bud's prelude entrance of growth beginning
Resists the connotation of
Shame implied.

The Lord's model of truth, sincerity,
Lends the ideal
Shared Relationship.
God given gift bestowed
That as friends.

Moreover, friendship returning, concerned interest,
One's own space of time, love in giving,
Stimulates gratification within a compelling need
To express verbally or with pen.

RETURNED LOVE

Agape' love superlative to the imagination
The encompassing grandeur of
Glorious Beauty within the universal sphere.

The incomparable, unconditional gift filled with
Grace, freedom, selflessness, and generosity,
God's Love.

No requirement expectation of sacrifice to receive
Yet our Lord's desire is our obedience
To attain His bountiful life established
From time's beginning and plan of provision.

Love the Lord your God with all your heart, mind, and strength.
Where is there space to find another's' love
Love for our children, spouse, friend.

How precious is that plan of origin.
The creation, salvation provision,
The love of God.
Christ's sacrificial love.
The assigned area of the soul, mind, will, and emotion,
For returning His love.
Throughout that exceptional bequest of friendship.

Loving God
Returned capacity for
Loving Each Other.

TWILIGHT REFLECTIONS

Come sit with me at evening twilight
See the array of colors
Becoming once again for another day passing
Disappearing as night surrounds us.

This moment of beauty enhances images of experiences recalled.
Bursting fireworks and their enthralling surge of felling
Sharing as another perceived the same.
Rising mountain peaks stretching toward spacious expanse
Within limited sight.
Rushing rivers meeting their own intersections to join
Greater water bodies for the designed destination.

Skyline, cloud formations, lavish floral clusters greenery display appear,
Then vanish.
There, another visionary! Scenery freshness and the brilliance of nature
Observed for a brief time before they dimly fade.

Wonderfully and these meditations
Comprehending thoughts intertwined with the concepts
Leading to peaceful places of euphoria.

May other times before sunset or sunrise occur
As we find gathering our thoughts, memories, hopes and dreams,
Fulfill God's expectation for our
Obedience in time of stewardship.

223

COMMITMENT

Darkness surrounds me.
Stillness and quiet join the peaceful suggested
Time of newness with appearance of light.
I welcome another wonderful
New Day Of Life.

Patiently awaiting thoughts to
Recall previous occasions,
It is almost startling to silently hear
I am happy!

Twice before along this journey
Happiness has intervened the existence of daily routine
Seemingly so mundane midst the unawareness of joy lacking.
Why Now?

Lying safely, warm, in need of no certain provision
Except for contentment following
Recent turmoil, doubt, confusion and guilt.

Now I am happy
For I have been affirmed, I am acceptable,
Self-worth confirmed.
I am loved.
Love, the source through which
True Happiness is Received.

RAINBOW OF PROMISES

A Son was promised. A Son was given.
He the only heir.
To the throne of Heaven.

A promise is a promise to be fulfilled.
And it was so.
Though the Son's absence in Heaven was ordained by
The Father
While our Lord visited earth.
Yet the planned purpose indwell Jesus
Found Him in favor with God
And He continued growing in obedience.

As the rainbow of colors blend
Many are the promises we are given
Only to receive to become co-heirs with Christ.

How majestically beautiful
This rainbow of colors in the sky to be seen and shared
By all.
The exquisite profusion distinctly expressing hope's
Beginning
Ending as designed to capture the awesome work of
Creation,
Promise, and purpose for man to know
The expanse of God's love.

God's vow is everlasting as the rainbow
Constant in shape, design, and color.

Jesus is the rock of our salvation
His Word is pure as
The rainbow is like no other.

MUSIC

Created composition intangible, yet an integral interspersing
Well enmeshed among the senses.
Melodious strains become visionary through one's
Sight of beauty
Perceived within fields of floral profusion.

Hear heart the arrangement of the
Score of rolling seas of scales
The solace of wind chiming notes
The thundering chords marvelously united in harmony.

Oh! The fragrant interlude of the soul's enraptured exhilaration
A rhapsody recalled.

Taste the symphony's delectable means permitting the sense of rhythm
Circulating other stimulated awareness of gratification.
Touch incomparable, phrasing becoming personal experience
To find its treasure chest for pleasurable reminiscence

God given sixth sense of sharing.
Can this explain our Lord's intention for
Music orchestration
Our privilege likewise to
Another give?

LIGHTHOUSE

As pain and sorrow persist, seemingly to remain,
Darkness pervades surrounding each change
In a new position
Difference in scenery or sanctuary for prayer.

Then hope's shadow flows over as a comforting cloud
To shelter from the all too heat of intensity.

One hears the song of a bird,
The Wind,
The Quiet.

Solace moves across and the feeling occurs as waves wash the shore
Returning to sea, and returning again,
And once more.

Oh! How peaceful the soul becomes
Flowing into time for moments of tranquility
Inspiring a season of praise and heartfelt joy.
That exaltation of the inward being.
Discomfort may occur with less intensity.
The hope of renewal gives meaning to the heart for strengthened faith.

Belief in God's Word of always being with you
Never forsaking His Loved Ones.

The Lighthouse
Always escorting your hope to change direction.
Turning and following Jesus
Wherever He Leads.

GOD GIVEN SENSITIVITY

In fear of the Lord there is strong confidence.
As strength fades and wanes
Faith exercised visualizes the
Truth of God's promise.
Our God remembers His Covenants.

Rejoice in the Lord.
His Word is true.
God is merciful.
Our Lord is mighty!
His Graciousness pervades.
Filling our very soul.

Hear the joyful sound of His glory.
Accept the fragrance of His intended healing.
Touch the spiritual reality of
His gift of life.
Taste the loving kindness of His goodness.
Seek the reverential fear of the Lord.
For He alone is worthy to be praised!

SHARING

Knowing my voice is heard.
Assurance my needs are understood.
Peaceful presence of
Intermingling thoughts with another.
Serenity in my heart's pain
Enjoined with the heart's pain of a loved one.
Exchanging smiles that needs no explanation.
Sighing with contentment in harmony.
Enjoying the same scenery.
Mutual respect midst disagreement through
The absence of anger.
Wishing to give likewise the twin
Belonging to my most treasured possession.
Acceptance of another
Not the same as I.
Offering one's deepest feelings
From the soul.
Sensing mutual joyfulness
Expressed through the exaltation of the
Inner spiritual being.
Simultaneously visualizing whatever
Our Heavenly Father
Will accomplish.
Trusting another with my greatest concern.
Contributing the source and revelation of my faith and strength.
Relying upon unending friendship.
Absorbing the warm rays together
Comparable to celestial light given to each for the other.
Extending your joy and petition for need required.

Rejoicing in time of need as well as
Rejoicing in time of abundance.
Sharing gives special meaning to love and friendship.
Sharing is a gift of love.

It is within the gift of sharing
We receive.

FRIENDS

Love at all times.
Accept each other without expectation of change.
Possess desirable character qualities.
Request revealing blind spots.
Commit to acquiring Christ like qualities.
Enjoy, rejoice and weep with each other.
Share beauty, song, and laughter.
Find pleasure in giving through self-expression,
Sharing and sacrificial time and tangible presentation.

FRIENDS

Disagree within the boundaries of truth, deference, and tolerance.
Request prayer and offer intercessory prayer.
Walk together spiritually
Trusting each other.

FRIENDS

Work together, play together, join in accordance with the same effort.
Listen patiently.
Speak cautiously.
Discern with spiritual guidance.
Counsel wisely with direction from the Lord.
Pray without ceasing.

I am grateful one of God's gifts
Is your friendship
And love.

Testimonials

I met Annette in 1968. We were in the same young adult Sunday school and training union class, and participated in the same church activities. Our friendship grew stronger and stronger as the years went by. I found Annette to be an attentive mother of three, a hard worker in the church and her home, and a great friend. She was so organized and always had a list of things to do, and always got everything done.

She is a great prayer warrior; she never gives up or quits until the problem is solved and the prayers are answered. (Some take years)

For years I had no idea that Annette was a writer until I received a poem from her on my birthday; it was beautiful. Inside the Annette I had known for years was an author wanting to be released, and now she has been released and what an author she is!

I love you much, Joyce

Annette Bryans is a gifted writer of this particular type of poetry using scripture passages as the basis for her writings. She has blessed friends and family on birthdays and other special occasions. Your readings of this poetry will be a blessing also.

Sara Eubanks, friend

When hearing the good news that Annette is publishing her book of poems, I was delighted. Her perseverance to accomplish her God given dream, has been amazing. She will bless many readers with her words of love and inspiration. So proud of you my friend.

Laura Motter

About Eleanor Annette (Wilson) Bryans
By Elyse Bryans

A native of Marietta, Georgia Annette has lived, worked, and raised her family in and around East Cobb County. A Charter Member of Eastside Baptist Church, she has faithfully studied and taught God's word and principles to multiple generations as a Christian Pre-School Teacher and Senior High School Girls' Sunday School Teacher. Hosting in-home weekly Bible Studies and volunteering in the Youth Ministry including serving as Chaperon on Summer Choir Tours - her example of a Godly Christian Woman became a legacy that many now consider to be a significant influence in their early Christian walk.

Annette discovered the joy of poetic free verse writing through composing handwritten greeting cards for friends and family. Encouraged by the response from these personalized cards, and with grown children in college and establishing careers while beginning families of their own - she expanded her daily writing discipline while enjoying time with her grandchildren. Currently, Annette is looking forward to retirement.

Eleanor Annette (Wilson) Bryans – Chronological Biography

February 15, 1938 Born in Marietta, GA when traffic circled town square passing second courthouse and what is now Shillings on the Square.

1944 Early School Days at Dodd Street Elementary in Marietta, GA

1945 – 1951 2nd through 7th Elementary Grades in Brookhaven, GA prior to that city's incorporation

1951 Began high school at Chamblee High, one of GA's Consolidated High Schools before moving cross county

1953 – 1954 Thomas Jefferson High in San Francisco, CA and moved farther northwest to Seattle WA

1955 – 1956 Graduated Grover Cleveland High in Seattle, WA

1956 Moved back to Marietta to marry GA High School Sweetheart – Robert (Bob) N. Bryans

Newlyweds joined Young Married Department at Roswell Street Baptist Church in Marietta, GA